JIGSAW

A Collection

F. Philip Holland

Patty's Original, 2006

P.Holland.

2

JIGSAW

*A Collection
of
poetry and prose*

by

F. Philip Holland

With illustrations by Pat Holland

Five-Bar-Gate Publishing

First published in 2012 by Five-Bar-Gate Publishing

ISBN 9780957361904

British Library Cataloguing in Publication Data: A catalogue record
for this book is available from the British Library.

Text ©F. Philip Holland 2012

Illustrations ©Pat Holland 2012

Printed and bound by Manchester Office Supplies,
Unit 2, Newby Road Industrial Estate,
Newby Road, Hazel Grove, Stockport, SK7 5DA
Tel: 0161 484 0001, Fax: 0161 484 0005
web: manchesterofficesupplies.co.uk

Distributed by Five-Bar-Gate Publishing,
1. Moorcroft, Lismore Road, Buxton, Derbyshire,
SK17 9GA, Tel: 01298 27644

4

- *Dedication* -

to Sir Christopher Ball,

a dear friend and fellow-poet.

*"Read this, and smile. One day I hope to find
the perfect line."*

John Elinger.

- *Acknowledgements and Thanks* -

To Roger Elkin, for kindly writing the Foreword to this book.
Roger has a long-established interest in the furtherance of poetry in general
for all people. He has been very involved in the world of literature for many
years: as a University tutor; an editor in the vanguard of poetry
publications; an esteemed judge in poetry competitions; a writer of
acclaimed critical commentary; an evergreen winner of poetry prizes; and
is nationally respected as a true poet with a plethora of published works. As
a friend he has encouraged me, and as a lecturer he has enlightened me.

To Linda Harry, yet again; for her patience and fastidiousness in helping
me to collate, paginate and design this book via that infernal thing called a
computer. Linda is creative, always calm when I am not, and as a true
friend is always helpful and encouraging in every possible way.

To Fiona Perry, my niece, for her literary, artistic and proof-reading
help. Being her favourite '*Avuncular*' in the tenacious study of the art of
Boggle and other fiendish word games, I could think of no-one better to
ask. Her help and competitiveness is greatly appreciated.

To those people and organisations who kindly asked me to give readings,
talks and performances: it is heartening to be given a platform from which
to communicate and entertain. More especially to those who commissioned
poems and were supportive of my endeavours. I beg forgiveness from those
friends, headed by Sir Christopher Ball, who have had to put up with
having various drafts slipped into their hands; have them appear on their
emails; been cajoled into reading and listening to these words; persuaded to
attend at various performances; and eventually been black-mailed into
accepting a copy as a gift, or even purchasing one for a doorstop.

Finally, to all my family for their love, help and tolerance.

Especially to Patty, not only for her sketches and illustrations, but for her
belief in me, and, most importantly, for her love and loyalty.

- *Foreword* -

"someone ought to write about this place,
cameras have no sense of smell"

So ends *Coming into Amsterdam* (pgs 47 - 49). That "*ought*"
carries the weight of significance, identifying Philip Holland's
commitment to his Muse. Throughout "*Jigsaw*", with its remarkable
variety of forms, styles, voices and subject matter, there is an underlying
sense of the poet trying to satisfy the need to do justice to his chosen
theme by marshalling his considerable battery of verbal skill to fashion
his acute awareness of the world around him, his sense of place,
character, creature and mood. This "need" results in a body of writing
that is accessible, comprehensible and approachable: poetry about real
things in a real world. Simultaneously, there is a richness of tone,
imagery, insight: almost every page carries a treasure trove. Philip
Holland is not afraid of using feeling: there's plenty of sentiment here
but very little sentimentality. There is seriousness, too, but without
being patronising, condescending or pretentious.

At the poetry's heart lies a love of words; and an ability to forge
these words into realisable and new images - sometimes overwhelming
in their richness, but always a product of the author's quest for accuracy
and insight. Take, for example, the opening of *'Coming into Amsterdam'*

Grey-wet mizzling;
darker clouds on bored, grey sky,
below, the rippling steely water.

On either side, in blunt procession,
come long, long and longer barges,
bluffing their stubborn stoicism,
seeming to low too low in the surface,
part of the element, sub-marinal.

> More barges, regular shoals of them,
> tidily-tied, like tinned fish.

The expression is exact and transparent; the scene precisely and economically captured; the full emphasis on the visual in complete harmony with what is being described. A particular feature of this poet's style is the use of compound/hyphenated words as seen in the opening line; as is the transferred epithet in the animistic "bored, grey sky" coupled with the "blunt procession" and "stubborn stoicism" of the barges; and the almost demotic note of "mizzling" and the cataloguing of "long, long and longer" which in no way prepare the reader for the comparison of the boats with fish, conveyed by the use of "shoals" and gloriously-realized in the verbal wit of the "tinned fish" simile. This is writing that opens doorways into perception; writing that shares the author's very special take on the world. Not persuaded? Then how about the later descriptions from the same poem;

> Farther off, whiter-grey-whiteness of new-age windmills,
> tri-winged like Dali-mutant albatross,
> or some Hitchcock nightmare gull.
> Slow-flapping their mesmeric energy;
> here, a fine balletic pointing to the sky,
> there, an agile pirouetting to the earth,
> now, a slant snatch at some bird-table roof.

What is remarkable is not only the referencing to the visual surrealities of Dali and Hitchcock in the similes, but also the precision in capturing the way in which the "slow-flapping" "mesmeric energy" of the windmills is pushed deliberately into focus via the use of "here...there...now...". Time and time again it is the mixture of the commonplace with the newly-coined that demands attention and admiration.

Favourite poems for me - mostly drawn from the celebration of the natural world or from Philip Holland's farming experiences - are similarly endowed:

Try *Weasel* (pg 24); *Swallow (*pg 25*); Curlew* (pg 32); *Foxfire* (pg 42); *Kite* (pg 52); *First Cockerel* (pg 73); *The Glevum Economy* (pg 91); *First Breath* (pg 89); *Wolf* (pg 94); *Sire* (pg 114); and *Gull* (pg 193). Written primarily in free-verse in a rich confection of the stylistic trappings of the poetry of D.H. Lawrence and Ted Hughes, the poems ripple with caught energy and a sense of wonder and wondrousness.

Requiem (pg 121) - one of only a few poems that makes direct reference to music - Philip Holland trained for many years in his youth as a concert pianist - plots the setting of the Latin text for the mass as prompted by hearing Duruflé's *Requiem* against the boy's drowning of "mewling kittens". The structural conceit is masterly and effectively resolved; as is made clear as the poet writes, "this day the boy will remember all his life". Similar craftsmanship is exhibited in poems that draw on dialect, complete with "translations", in a 21st century Hardyesque manner (see *Th'owd Mill,* pg 124); or in those written using metre and pure rhyme in regular quatrains (see *The Colonel*, pg 102) in an imitation of Betjeman's style.

But these nominated poems are only a sample of the wealths of this collection! There is much more to enjoy, to savour and to rejoice at in these poems: truly, poetry for all folk and for all occasions. They will repay repeated and careful reading, revealing new wonders at each new dipping.

I hope that you enjoy them as much as Philip obviously has in the "ought" of their writing!

Roger Elkin

- *Introduction* -

I'm probably best described as a retired hill farmer who writes, or rather tries to write, poetry. I was born in Buxton in a year that qualifies me for Winter fuel allowance. After a fairly poor showing at school I joined the family farm, whilst simultaneously studying privately to become a concert pianist. The latter wasn't totally successful. Later, after the D.I.Y. renovation of several houses, I became an hotelier for fourteen years, whilst still farming. Finally retiring from agriculture, owing to ill-health, I went to Derby University as a mature student to study for an English and Creative Writing Degree. Currently, I'm a part-time jeweller in partnership with my wife, Pat, ...and still trying to write poetry.

All my years on the land were spent at the family farm, "Glutton Grange", near Earl Sterndale. This is a place about five miles south of Buxton in the upper reaches of the River Dove, in an area that is now known as the White Peak of Derbyshire. My paternal family has farmed in the parish continuously for seven generations. From about 1600 my mother's family farmed around Sheen, just over the Derbyshire border in the Staffordshire Moorlands. My Great-grandmother's family, Kinder, (at one time de Kyndre, coming from the old Celtic word *Chendre*), lived and farmed around Kinder Scout in the Dark Peak continuously since 1385. Given these deep localized roots (and my rapidly increasing collection of birthdays) I'm guessing, and certainly hoping, I'll probably not be moving anywhere else now.

My primary education was at the village school of Earl Sterndale, afterwards at Buxton College Grammar School. I left school at sixteen with sparse and poor 'O' levels. In hindsight - that useless tool so frequently found too late - I think that I probably went to the wrong school; Maths and Sciences, which is what my particular Grammar school excelled in, were ever mysteries to me. I only wanted to study Literature, which was slightly frowned upon there; Art, also considered an unnecessary indulgence, and Music, which wasn't even taught at all. I was the first boy in the history of the school to take Music 'O' level, for which I had to study privately.

With typical belligerence I often purposely got myself thrown out of class so I could sneak off to the School Hall to practice on a greatly-under-used Bechstein grand piano. The frequency of these perverse actions always increased whenever a Music Festival or Exam that I was entered in was imminent. Of course my Headmaster knew what was going on, but to his credit, and my undying gratitude, he never admonished me once. Occasionally he would open the Hall door, look in for a brief moment, and then simply carry on. A few times he did sit and listen properly. I pretended not to see him; I think he pretended I wasn't there.

I wonder now if perhaps he subconsciously acquiesced to that maxim: *'Lead a child in the way in which he will go'* ?

At the end of my secondary education I well remember my Careers Master telling me to: "*...go home, farm and grow fat*". Although I did indeed take most of that advice for the next forty years, I also did one or two other things along the way.

I began piano lessons at the age of five; my family having always been very drawn to music and the Arts in general. Music, singing, poetry and drama were encouraged throughout the wider family. On my father's side three brothers married three sisters from a neighbouring village, so it was no surprise that myself, both my siblings and twelve Holland cousins all met up at Festivals over many years. My father was a keen amateur painter in both watercolour and oils. My maternal grandmother was a trained singer who once performed in the Free Trade Hall in Manchester. She was also an early supporter of Women's Suffrage, and a vanguard female student at Rease Heath College in Cheshire in the late 1890s.. She was ever a great influence and encouragement to me.

After leaving school I continued to study piano, together with my sister, Joan, with the legendary Fanny Waterman of Leeds. The intension was for us to become concert pianists as duettists, and we were indeed semi-professional for some time - whilst still farming! We appeared at the 1969 Harrogate Festival of Arts and Science, gave recitals in Leeds Town Hall, were Runners-up in the 1969 Royal Overseas Music Competition in London, and competed successfully in most of the Music Festivals in the North-West and Midlands. We were also fortunate to be broadcast on the radio from the B.B.C.'s Milton Hall in Manchester But by the time I was twenty-one I realized that music was not going to be my chosen life.

Later, my first wife, Kathryn, and I, with our two children, Elizabeth and Edward, owned and ran Swainsley Hall. This was an idyllic place near Butterton in the Manifold Valley which we had made into a Country House Hotel, and where we lived for fourteen years - again, whilst still farming! It was a gloriously hectic and happy time, marred only by Kathryn's illness. Sadly, she died at an early age; all other odious minor problems paled into insignificance. Only the love and support of my two teenage children and wider family saved me from contemplating suicide. It was a dark time indeed.

However, I'm now very happily re-married, to Pat, my other soulmate. I know how fortunate and blessed I am to have met her. Pat has had more than her share of tragedy in her former lives. Being married to her is simply just wonderful. Together with our collective total of six children, their partners and eleven grandchildren, life is complete again.

Curiously, we have been together now for longer than with our previous spouses. I still help out some days a week in Pat's jewellery business in the centre of Buxton.

In 2001 I was diagnosed with signs of muscular dystrophy. This, together with the parlous state of British Agriculture at that time, was both persuasive and absolute; I chose to retire from farming. Suddenly, with so much time to fill, I began to write. Then, after a wonderful holiday in Rome in April of the same year, being mesmerized by the contents of the Villa Borghese, especially the statues by Bellini, I began to write poetry. Something I hadn't done since school days. Soon I had self-published two anthologies, which, to my surprise and great satisfaction, quickly sold out. Two further anthologies, a 'Concise Derbyshire Dialect Dictionary' and a first 'Collection' of poetry followed over subsequent years.

In 2005, prompted and persuaded by Pat, I decided on a challenge: exploring the chance of Further Education as a mature student. This was to be at the soon-to-be-opened Devonshire Dome campus of Derby University in Buxton.

Quite by chance at the first Open Day I met a gentleman called Christopher Ball. We chatted amiably and soon discovered that we had a shared interest in Derbyshire, education and, especially, poetry - and that we both tried to write the latter. I persuaded him that it might be interesting if, as keen amateur poets, we exchanged some work for mutual constructive criticism. We did.

Imagine my acute embarrassment when attending the Enrolment Day some weeks later, a certain Dr. Richard Tresidder commented that he remembered seeing me: "…talking to Sir Christopher Ball, our Chancellor, at the Open Day"…"Who?..." immediately froze on my lips. I had unwittingly had the temerity to comment on the work of someone I knew merely as Christopher; someone I originally thought might be considering becoming a mature student like me, blithely unaware of his Chancellorship of the premises at which I was about to enrol! But, to my good fortune, we are still exchanging poetry and giving critique to one another's work seven years later…although I am furiously jealous that he has won more prizes in poetry competitions than I have!

Nevertheless, I am honoured and delighted that we share this love of words and their weaving into poetry. This is why I dedicate my second collection to him. Christopher has always been a very great support and influence to me; he remains an honest and candid critic of my work; and most importantly he is a very dear friend.

After three very tough years at University, with numerous moments of self-doubt, despair and contemplated withdrawal, but always with the great support of my tutors, I managed to graduate with a 2:1 B.A. Hons. in English & Creative Writing. I had tried very hard; it wasn't so bad for an old farmer who had: "…*gone home, farmed and grown fat.*"

Ah, Mr. Careers Master where are you now? I would love to tell you how I still enjoy literature, music and art, how I am still fascinated by words and their infinite inter-twinings, how I still revel in reading, speaking, and listening to poetry… and how I am still trying to write it!

My poetry was once described by one old friend as eclectic. I always say that is a posh word meaning difficult to categorize or, to put it bluntly, mixed. I like to compose in many forms and styles: classical, contemporary, rhyming, free-verse, sonnet, ballad, haiku, prose, parody and local dialect. My inspiration comes from many sources: nature and the countryside, music, art, history, literature, people, travel, and various life experiences.

In this second collection it will be apparent to both the most flitting and the most fiercely critical reader that I write at vastly differing depths and intensities, and could be accused of being rather indulgent on some themes. Whether this is by conscious or subconscious choice, chance, whim, lack of control or just adventurousness I can't, or perhaps shouldn't, conjecture upon. Suffice it to say that the end results are always bounded by inspiration, imagination, word choice, and to what degree of talent the reader may confirm, or deny, I may have.

But I do try to accept brickbats as well as praise.

The title to this Collection is *"Jigsaw"*. All the pieces are from what I will call *occasions* in my life. Some are physical observations, others are brief thoughts. Some are poignant memories, others are a shade satirical. There are travel descriptions, figments of imagination, and true records. A few may be lightly amusing and others are quite dark. I haven't grouped them, as in my first *'Collection'*, they are, I suppose... *eclectic*?

None fit exactly into any place or pattern with their neighbour, yet all complete a poetic adventure that is representational of my writing: part real, part surreal; part collage, part montage; part impressionist, part concrete. If you look at any one piece of jigsaw it is complete in itself, but is also part of a bigger picture. Perhaps my jigsaw is multi-dimensional - like a Rubik's cube? If so, then there are certainly some scratched and some missing tiles.

Where I have used dialect, uncommon words, or subjects which might possibly provoke interest and offer explanation, there are *'Notes & Glossary'* and *'References'* sections at the end of the book. I hope that they may be useful.

In conclusion. Words are like stars for me. It is wonderful to have millions of them and, depending where you are, there are infinite patterns to look at. But, unlike some stars, words are not fixed; and when chosen with care, cherished and treated with respect and love, they can become fascinating when cast into poetic jigsaws.

So please share my words, even read them aloud. And if you want to know more of yourself, may I urge you to try writing some of your own.

I hope that you may enjoy some part of this book.

Yours aye,

F. Philip Holland.

- CONTENTS -

Jigsaw

Opening up the box of my jig-sawed life
I look at the pieces; jumbled and fragmented,
each piece a time, some event, a day used up.
This jigsaw needs sorting out, making sense of.
Or, if some pieces missing, the picture incomplete,
I will have to pause and make some more to finish it.
Each piece is vital; I cannot do without even one of them.
Although I can never be sure how many more I will need.

First, I look for cornerstones, they are so important;
childhood, parents, siblings, growing, learning, life.
Next, all the straight-edged ones, those stepping stones;
rules, conditions, seasons, paths, crossroads, and decisions.
Then those that perhaps need fitting on some other side;
false starts, mistakes, denials, disappointments, regrets.
My outline is complete; I begin to look for the next pieces,
some harder than others, love, loss, gain, death.

My youth became middle-aged, then older, some wisdom grasped,
All the experiences of work, budget, debt, rewards, and failure;
resolve cemented; yet boundaries breached and excuses employed.
Good and bad days stringing along my abacus, slowly totalling.
Bright and dull colours, long hours of summer madness,
gaudy shades of equinox, and iron of Wintertime.
My pieces, like small chameleons, scutter into place,
they interlock as perfectly and firmly as my DNA

The joy, and annoyance, of cherry-blossomed boughs
that try my eyes and patience in one small corner.
The multiplications of leaves and grass and walls, the
impossibilities of cathedral skies, the quiet consternation

in a spreading lake; my scene is filling to an understanding.
Here, the figures form, with gesture, smiles and frowns.
The pieces link, their tabs and mouths a geometric code
determined by time and place, reactionary braille of memory.

Some odd pieces mystify, they thwart and confuse, reject
my incessant turning round and over as I scour the board.
Did I really go there? see this? say that? and why?
These are the pieces that are hard to quantify, difficult
in assimilation, and yet they have their place of course.
Some pieces I would prefer not to include, and yet
my picture, and thus my life, is not true without them.
Perhaps a little paring with my pocket knife? Oh no!

My picture must not lie; these pieces must have integrity,
they were painted in their time, and have some record.
Like any tapestry, the wool and shading must comply;
my pen and fingers are the needles stitching in consideration.
These pieces are a blueprint for what has already happened,
the days grow bright in a mirroring remembrance.
Yet now I am so loathe to finish what I started
and wish there were more spaces in the frame to fill.

And so, shall I liken it to a kind of mosaic of old marble?
or a vague pointillist piece of art, with all those flecks?
My jigsaw is like a tattoo, a living, pixelated ink design,
or perhaps a Turkish rug with thousands of those double knots.
Each point of reference, each intricate pattern, each shape,
a part completeness, but nothing till it links to make the whole.
For if you want to know me better, inspect these pieces;
each one, each day, each thought and each occasion.
These are some hours of my existence; they may explain my life.

Baltic Dawn

Sun to port.
South-east from Copenhagen.
Our sea has no waves,
merely the slightest of sluggish, oozing movements,
black as molasses, or stirred warm tar.

On the brimmed horizon,
the surface burning, dripped down from the soldering sun,
lie brown-orange weals, stretching the ocean's flayed back.

Around us, seven ships
trudging their trade, like ticks on hide.

Moon to starboard;
an imprint from the ghosted half-night,
the dark-day-night,
like a lino cut in the cool, grey west.
No stars, all dissolved, assimilated.

Land, way over; not visible,
but proved by a faint, slender chimney stack,
its distant wisp of pollution
seeping from an invisible top.

Two ships seem to collide, pass, and break free,
the illusion shattered.

Churned salt to stern,
breaking the black mantle
to show white water dragged from below,
a frothed wakefulness
of ancient charts and passages.

No wind, no wings, no canvas.

Yet I can hear in the plashing,
dim echoes of sea-songs
from a far, foreign tongue,

a waking of old sailors
and fish.

Solmonath

In Solmonath there are no shadows,
       drab landscape merges into sky.
Mists blur down to soft solidity,
       horizons rank with arcing rain.
Leaden banks hang over water,
       a heaving dross that somehow floats.
Gaunt hillsides threaten silent thunder,
       meadows drench in mercury.
Weak sunlight struggles hopelessly,
       a ghostly whiteness barred by walls.
Broken crossbars from some old field gate,
       half-sunken in morass of mud.
Pock-marked by puddle's dark infection,
       the chommered lane leads nowhere now.
Bruised by Winter's harsh besiegement,
       grey, tortured tussocks chained in rime.
This half-light, no-time season wearies,
       each scrap-yard tree a blackened hulk.
Chill-gripping hask of bitter wind,
       no shadows seen in Solmonath.

Weasel

A flash of red and white!
    Alarm to the patient thrush.
    Even the hawthorn's palisade
    of spears becomes a poor defence,
    thick ivy battle-camouflage has no effect.
    The dry-walled buttresses are breached by stealth.

Squirming slither of alizarin!
    Scant tail that ends in shorter death.
    The truce of belly-whiteness becomes deceit,
    invokes an ambush from supreme surveillance,
    keen-nosed evolution merely grants the gluttony.
    His ritual dance concludes in sanguine coup-de-grace.

Madder! How he gorges on the blood!
    Sucks and licks the fragile shells to silence,
    drains the skins to dust, wrecks in lusted frenzy.
    His cut-throat knives allow no mercy, no remorse,
    leave a ruin even squandering pirates could not excel.
    He wraps his sated fur away to rest without a conscience.

Rank, ravaging pernicity!
    God forgot to give him shame,
    and Satan hands him no restraint.
    He lies and preens with carefree paws,
    then snoozes in replete and selfish disregard.
    And cannot comprehend his natural malevolence.

Swallow

Your un-timed arrival
advances the speaking clock,
    brings consternation to Tannoy systems.

        Your twittering code
          makes Soviet bugs ineffective,
      listening to a scrambled enigma in remorse.

Your blue and white,
copied to svelte mannequins by Saville Row suitors,
    marries haute couture to formal tails.

        Your mud-mortared nurseries
     cling cheekily to mock-Tudor eaves, drop business cards
          on the stock-broker's Jaguar.

Your flocking abacus
revolts electricity wire's geometry, preened tuning forks
    become a crossed-line disharmony on the telephone.

        Your dare-devil manoeuvres
      show no fear, bring emulation from Red Arrows,
   yet, cautiously, they still pack their parachutes.

Your flawless migration
confounds Mercator's clumsy charts, needs no Sat-nav,
    knows no post code, brings an envy from the stay-at-homes.

Metamorphosis

Two halves.
Or are they really two half-submerged wholes?
Twin wing-tips of some gigantic butterfly?
Head, thorax, abdomen and legs buried deep,
deep in the Derbyshire landscape.

The largest specimen ever found?
Some palaeontologist's dream come true?
Wing-beats louder than a Sikorsky.
Spielbergian in nightmare phantasy.

No. Not a butterfly.
No flitting from tree to tree.
No wing-tracery veining of primordial Summer
Not a giant Kafka insect caught in cooling amber,
nor a mawkish Victorian specimen speared and forgotten.

Just winding wheels;
bisected, cut up rather, set in dull, gross concrete,
an epitaph of failed commerciality, a quick fix of redundancy.
Useless emblems of culture and community dis-spiritedness.
Chained down, emasculated, painted-up in garish colours,
ridiculed with flowery borders, more like fairground wreaths.

Winding wheels;
lacking only the plaqued list of casualties, the fallen-forgotten.
No death-reasoned certificates: emphysema; arthritis;
pneumoconiosis; such pretty words…

Winding wheels;
iron gossamer spread above the hardened arteries of hell.
Coal-angel's wings; past-shunning, fossilized,
birthing coal, burying men…

Winding wheels;
set up in dishonourable monument,
lest we forget, lest we cease to remember all that sweat,
all that dust, the coughing and the crooked backs...

And the old miner shakes his head
at his energy bill and Winter fuel allowance.
Looks through his kitchen window
and swears at them in their inertia.

Miss Morrissey

(First Voice)

I hear that Miss Morrissey's dead and gone!
How sad she's come to the end of her days,
she certainly did have some old-fashioned ways.
Oh, we'll miss those terrible whalebone stays,
and her sensible shoes, that always shone.
Those hand-knitted dresses, her sweaters home-spun,
that handbag, her features all wrinkled and wan.
She used to perform in those amateur plays,
we'll miss all her funny old blue-stocking ways,
and the awful shock of her permed-hair days.
With twin-set and pearls, or beige cardy on,
they'll not replace Morrissey, now that she's gone.

(Second Voice)

Miss Morrissey worked until seventy-one
in '*Accounts*', and never once asked for a raise.
Never rude, or would think to expect any praise,
"*Good morning!*" on even the dreariest of days.
She always poured tea from her silver on trays,
and, disapproving of '*scone*', she said '*scon*',
her father, she said, was an old Oxford Don,
what a shame Miss Morrissey's finally gone.
Kept herself to herself for most of her days,
never married and spurned any ardent Don Juan.
She never was known to have any fun,
and Office Parties would always shun.
She often kept cats, though most were just strays,
but it's sad that she's come to the end of her days.

(Third Voice)

Well, I have a secret, but don't pass it on;
when I was a youth, but with older men's ways,
Miss Morrissey and I had a brief liaison.
But we parted and both went our separate ways,
yet I never forgot those fond, faraway days.
Years later we met, though both had moved on,
when she quietly told me she'd named our child, John.
She had him adopted, discreet and anon,
and stayed spinster, alone, and set in her ways.
I still love her, and will, till the end of my days.
So I'll hide all my grief and just carry on,
but I'll miss Miss Morrissey, now that she's gone.

Snail and Shell

How easily you glide along the garden path's worn slate,
      a damp May afternoon's slow-motioned marathon.
Swirled amber-yellow patterning of your circles,
      such fragile armour to the thrush's maul.
Fine domicile; gentle whirlpool, shellac lustred, soft-slowing.

Now the limestone coper's fossil of your past relates,
      a grey-white coal millennia.
Spun skeleton's relief of earlier coral time,
      such resistance to the waller's knap.
Slime trail; frilled edges, stretching horns, slow-sliding.

How your sensitivity contracts inside your shell, retreats
      in horror at my testing finger.
Attacking pagan to the sealed and spiralled vulva,
      such monstrous inquisition to the Spring.
Sweet sloth; soft jaws, slow browse, tender-stroking.

Now the beauty of your sensile movement captivates,
      a shy modesty in glorious birth.
Your scalloped cradle from the warm sea,
      such gentle lifting of the Venus.
Translucent skin; delicate expand, soft contract, moist-curling.

How the heavens hold you in your spinning, rotates
      red Mars in vain pursuing of those cycles,
a barren courtship in the slow sustain of time.
      Here the snail collides the two, hermaphrodite
completeness; unicorn and cornucopia, snail and shell, lui et elle.

Rope

Caked boots, tacked hands;
links to earth and the hovering horizon of rope.
In between come joining knots of sinew
thickly curled around the stubborn bones.
Some grins, some scowls, no fuss,
and always that supreme and concentrated effort.
Teams: Norton, Bosley, Two Dales, Sheen, and more.
Comrades, rivals, athletes, friends, and more,
but only before and after, never during.
Oh no! During the stretch and grind
nothing signifies except the winning;
that whistle of short, sharp blast to the victor!

Inked numbers smudge on bulging thighs,
team-names display across broadened backs.
Belts, buckles, bootlaces, socks and sweat.
This short-cropped field of sandy loam becomes
a temporary battlefield, though no blood spilt,
just a draining of the nobly-vanquished.
Their fore-fathers; Romans, Vikings, Normans, Celts,
all met again in tournament that leaves no flag planted;
this yielding land is, and was, already theirs.

Instruction; "*Pick up the rope, Take the strain, Pull!*"
Two sets of bulldogs with the creaking meat.
A surge, stagger, warning, deadlock, ...waiting.
But still those pit-prop legs refuse to give,
a mined honour, dredged from the ultimate.
Eventually the vices tighten, then a slow dance in unison,
chanting, step-synchronized, backwards to the win!
Such an ironic reversing to fortune.

Those vital wooden pegs and coloured tapes
that first lined up, now no longer agree.
The other team inched slowly forward to defeat.

Best of three, and three cheers doubled!
New scores counted, old scores settled.
Yet good-natured promises for the next time.
Just like those earlier cherished tilting-yards,
the sagging tent and twin-ploughed furrow
abandoned for the medals' tape and chink,
and the laughing Blacksmith's Arms!

Rubáiyát

I

Your lambent eyes are like a thousand stars,
and worth the weight of countless golden bars!
My rival's blood grows cold that late I spilled,
to prove my love, I'll show my jealous scars!

II

Sweet fool! When wine is tasted at late hour,
and love forever promised with one flow'r,
then all admirers you may have. But scorn
my honest heart, then love of thine may sour!

III

Awake! The morning flies from night's dark hold,
and feathered chorus rings like false Fool's gold!
Though he has held you sleeping these small hours,
his yesternight's hot words will soon grow cold!

Curlew

Odd mixture of elegance, sobriety and mournfulness.

Legs half-borrowed from some off-course stork,
drab mottlings of a lesser-fashioned textile reject,
vibrato that persuades the impresario to shudder,
and the beak? Unfortunate, to say the least.

Here: where peat and rush sway hand in hand,
in rank, moving sponge of woeful mists, heath-bounded,
where chilling winds blow and sough till all is frayed,
as if to emanate the very calls of solitude and sorrow,
this creature is placed to act upon the Moorlands watch.

Is it a portent for the future, or a ghost that cannot rest?
Why do I loathe and love its sparse presence in my life?

I have no jealousy of this sentinel post. Nor the privacy
it guards so well, yet cannot defend, in spite of all the weapons
in its arsenal; winds, distance, height, and rain, and rain, and rain.

To find a nest, now there's a rarity. Blotched unroundnesses,
these shells a shape of river-worn stones and just as dull to see.
A scratched depression, half-hearted, not even built as home.
Spareness of comfort, draughty, singular, and yet so very curlew;
thrift-threadbare, parsimonious and always crying; "Woe is me!"

Bramble-bankrupt, languishing in those quaint, half-semi-tones.
The slim scimitar of its bill no hussar-threat, no bravado,
just a curved grubbing-stick in lonely marsh and moor.
And always the wail and wail and wail of worried lamentation.

Those great, open skies above become an echoing membrane
to the morose and lachrymosity. A hollowness to the requiem.

Job's comforter! Warbling like the newly-widowed,
or the keening widower. Wet gorse a spiteful wreath of loss.

Yet shall I answer in a muted mockery? Or shall I also weep?

Watch

"…I've over-wound…
found it in his drawer…
…sure I put it in my purse…
worse now he's gone…dear Fred…"

"Has it been stopped long?"
"…wrong?... oh no, it's just old…
told me to leave it there…
…where is it?…I put it in my bag…"

"Is it a battery watch?"
"…watch?...yes, it belonged to Fred…
dead for years…can't seem to find…
…wind it up at all…can't see...ah, here it is!…"

"When was it last going?"
"...slowing? No, it's stopped…
dropped it once…belonged to Fred…
…bedside table it was…in his drawer, his things..."

"It might just need a clean and service."
"…service?...yes, it was his firm's service watch…
watch for forty years work…long term…
…firm bought it for Fred…he's dead, you know..."

"You have to remember it's a very old watch"
"…watch?...oh yes, it's his… ah, here's my stick…
'stick it in the drawer', he said …found it today…
…May it was, he died…in his sleep... dear Freddy..."

"We'll have to send it away."
"...in May?...yes, he died in May...
day after his retirement...we were going away...
...may I leave it with you?...now, where's my bag?

"We'll ring you when it's ready."
"...Freddy's?... yes, it isn't going...
growing older... forty years he worked...
...worked all his life...just for a watch... ah well..."

"We'll do our very best."
"...test?...oh yes, test it...
it might just be the winding...
...finding it difficult...have we had Christmas?..."

P. Holland.

Tell me a story

You look sad.
Sat still, clutching your best-loved toy,
the oldest and grubbiest one you have.

You look like me.
You look as though all the daisies have wilted
and drooped, and you have lost your favourite story-book.

I'll come and sit beside you, tell you a story.
Put my arm around you, tell you about the forty thieves
and the little Ali Baba.

I'll tell you that you remind me of someone who's not here
and that you look like her, as well as me.
Tell you that she loved you just as much as I do.

Tell you about a little girl who grew up too soon,
someone who lost part of her childhood.
Tell you that you can always come and talk to me.

One day I'll say that I give you away to someone else.
You will love him even more than you love me,
and he will love you even more than I can.

Your children will love you even more than I can.
I'll tell you that you are making your own stories now,
not to complete mine, but to continue yours.

I'll tell you that when you have your children
you must tell them this story.
It may help you, and them.

One day I'll say how sorry I am to be going away,
but that I'll come back from time to time,
if you want me to. I'll be here in these words.

One day my story will be ended.
You will make your own.
There is so much paper to write on.

Equus

Religion fails for the realists;
their Gods prove false, let them down,
the gold masks slip and crumble.

Ask the oddball, fervent in his passion,
what the motive is; or was; where the reasoning.
Ask the psychiatrist, he with the disembowelling
technique, the cutting-in to see what purpose.
Ask the failing relationships, the Greek tragedies,
about the lies, the over-riding real emotions,
the under-mining selfishness, the deep jealousies.

The all-seeing eyes have been turned to the front,
religiously fixed, looking for the next, new horizons;
those that come thundering through the dreams,
those terrified imaginings, the stark truths.

Youth hurts; is an earth-bound yoke,
a cross that stretches and bleeds dry,
a gifted wooden horse impossible to ride.
The whys and theory come as no absolvement.

This free-riding centaur gallops through the nightmare,
needing only one pair of eyes; the sublime master's.
The insight of the blind coursing on the blinded.

Even the expert is blinkered by his experiences.
The mind is captive only to the scope of things.

Does science understand spirituality?
Discuss ad infinitum.

Funny

Funny how love can know
So funny how love can grow
It's funny how love can say hello
Funny how love can go

    And it's funny why love has shining eyes
    So funny why love takes wing and flies
    It's funny why love can wear disguise
    Funny why love tells lies

Funny how love can make you glow
So funny how love can answer no
It's funny how love can sink so low
Funny how love goes slow

    And it's funny why love is full of sighs
    So funny why love can spring surprise
    It's funny why love is never wise
    Funny why love soon dies

Funny how love won't last the day
So funny how love can fade away
It's funny how love is hard to say
Funny how love turns grey

    And it's funny why love seems long ago
    So funny why love can drag you low
    It's funny why love won't let you go
    Funny why I love you so

        ....Funny why I love you so…

Boy on a stone trough

It's a picture of me
sat on a trough,
aged about three,
in the old lambing croft.

Dressed in my shorts
surrounded by pigs,
smiling my thoughts
as they root and dig.

Black scuffled shoes
without any socks,
a bruise on my leg,
some childhood knock.

I remember that time
looking back there,
now an older clock chimes
and there's winter in my hair.

Yew

Dark, dark your green.
Ancient of the churchyard.
Your cool depths of dense frond and shredded fingers
smelling of the centuries.
Occasionally glimpsing black branches,
silent shadows through the darkest hue,
echoing the bowmens' ghosts.
Your rancid poison shot through the greenery.
Dark, dark your secret.

Still, still your presence.
Warlord of the battlefield.
Sprung spirits of a man's height and another's length
joined by the shattering arrow.
Your roots feeding on the bowmens' sleep,
shading the bones that returned.
Sons laughing at the green of Spring,
then silent in Winter's black.
Still, still your secret.

Quiet, quiet your growing.
Keeper of the hour-glass.
Dark red your berries' blood, the bowmens' harvest
spilling in the screams of war.
Your poisoned beads and new-flecked wounds
linked in the dance of death.
Leaving wives to weep in empty beds,
girls tending their young mens' graves.
Quiet, quiet your secret.

Dark, still and quiet.
Your release to a thousand quivers,
       your witness to a thousand mounds.
       your ears to a thousand sermons.
Strange, this tree of Albion stands so revered,
symbol of war enshrined in hallowed ground.
Poison in the chalice, blood in this field of peace,
the red of death on the evergreen of life,
       living mortality.

Slow Burn

Dead engines, bent girders, machinery, old guttering...
Drab liturgy of scrap-yard, gripped in the cancer of rust.
Here's the waiting chaos, and here's the moistened air,
but where's the spark? the flames? the smoke and ash?
Yet here's a grim, slow burning of metal recalcitrants
who will not, cannot, repent their man-made sins today.

Gas cookers, cast-iron railings, out-dated filing cabinets...
Naturally absolving. Unholy conflagration of silent fires.
Here, massed metal dumbly screams, an acrid smell of rottenness,
purgatorial beaded sweat, disaffection with designer obsolescence.
Flayed skins peeling, flaking, the foul flesh drips slowly off,
chassis bones crack and drop, the rank blood-oil drains quietly away.

Twisted pipes, corrugated sheets, signs from motorway...
Slowest cremation; that depressing grasp of invisible flame.
Here, the final Inquisition of crass modes and paltry gadgets.
This cankered furnace-pouring, longer, stronger, than the first.
Is this all that we can promise? What value scrappage now?
Work and some brief use is just the price we have to pay.

Wire meshing, dead cats-eyes, shopping trolleys, grids...
This all-devouring process allows no pardon, no escape.
Here the disease is pan-endemic, here the treatment arbitrary, no
matter how we paint and galvanize, steam-clean, protect with grease.
Re-cycling? A temporary delay. Jealous earth reclaims its ore.
We only borrow, smelt, construct, tear down and cast away.

Iron Maiden, Model T, Ark Royal, Concorde, AK-47...
Throwing rockets at some distant moon or planet can do no good.
There we grossly make a graveyard in the heavens. Some sky-burial
without those efficient Himalayan vultures, or chant, or prayer.
Our great ideas are piling up in space. Through telescopes our
revolving rubbish looks down on our decay. Rust will have its way.

Foxfire

There is that lope, that running trot,
as if the paw tracks burned them at their heels;
the old fable proved.

Two foxes, red-earthed, ruddy,
coming from the close, night-prisoned wood,
their flamed fur, scorched tip of tail, just visible.

The chilling dim backdrops an eerie theatre,
a rising-moonlight barely warms their courting place.
Flashed split-second of her backward glance,
and he, stilled, frozen, a forward hungered glare.

Smoke-white chests thump, and gingered edges
of soft bellies sear on their fleet-foot, sly-marauding need.

There is that burning power in her eyes,
she pauses, turns again, the slightest hesitation.
This feint argument no case against her scent,
which signals to the cudgel of his sanguine brain.

Faint wisps of condensation steam
from his lolled and most blood-thirsty tongue,
which, like a swift, red rag, quick-slips over slim jowls.
those tearings at temporary rest, this hunger is more keen.

He must engage; the vixen tells him so,
screaming in her want of Spring,
a thin, high, eldritch yelp of heat.
His counterpoint: a tandem bark.

But as we peer, as thrilled and silent statues,
the embers of their conflagration disappear,
their ashes melt away; disdain to our awareness.
The masks that were, suddenly not even there.

And in the silent, blue-black sky
only a pallid moon remains,
like ice on fire.

Aubade

I stumble in glass-shattered sleep,
thoughts raging to the edges of my skull
persistently wreaking their maelstrom,
images hammering into no sense, full
strengthened in a jumbling bedlam;
like nervous, slaughter-housed sheep.

I shrink from these nightmares,
clown-cavorting in a mêlée of circus,
hideously laughing their squander,
hazed in the grey-ghost wakefulness
of drawn curtains, an opaque meander
imprisoned by sly-softened snares.

Waiting, then waking to the release:
that first bird-call; the paper-cart's
humming rise and fall, a batteried life;
a door-slam of commuting car; footsteps'
advancing rhythm under avenued leaf;
the clack of letterbox; a normalcy to peace.

And should I not have guessed,
as night follows day follows night,
that defiance to reality is futile?
I might not have seen another flight
of morning wings; a knowing smile
of recognition; some sympathy depressed.

And seamlessly this torrid dawn
links, spins the day from blanking night;
a time-and-motioned live routine;
a fading-up of colours, sound and sight;
a happy rigmarole from snoreless libertine,
as dew fades, drying on the rose and lawn.

Glad to be in untormented calms
of work, and things to contemplate;
the switching-on of toast and tea,
news of floods in Pakistan, some latent
movement of the mortgage rate, see
moors and smell the stoic, widening farms.

So quick, this daybreak birth,
spontaneous as the turning tide,
in spite of covering clouds,
a doleful moon that nearly cried.
I join the morning-solemn crowds,
glad to feel the light, the sobered earth.

The day is to hand and sky glows
slowly white. Grey buildings smile,
put on their make-up; glossed wood
and mirrored glass, red doors, blue tile.
A hum of traffic creeps and stalls. Could
men release themselves from factory woes?

The streetlight's orange fades and stops,
a cheaper, brighter naturalness takes on.
Only a Volvo, more cautious than the others,
shines a smug perverse of headlight woebegone,
an über-safety to chattering Nursery mothers.
The jackdaws look askance from chimney-pots.

A blocking hill keeps back the infant sun,
its light now pawned to blushing cloud.
But, dropping down in eastward pull,
this stubborn mass is not allowed
to hinder what is rightly, fair and full,
to manifest itself when once begun.

And I, paused, reflect on last
night's labyrinth of fear,
cannot shrug it off as phantasy,
and wonder if this next, near
sleep will be more easy,
a blindness to eyes shut fast?

But no matter.
No morbid night can argue strong
when dawn light finally comes along,
its prison-shatter.
Come night, come light, dark or burn,
asleep, awake, turn on turn.

Coming into Amsterdam

Grey-wet mizzling;
darker clouds on bored, grey sky,
below, the rippling, steely water.

On either side, in blunt procession,
come long, long and longer barges,
bluffing their stubborn stoicism,
seeming to lie too low in the surface,
part of the element, sub-marinal.

More barges, regular shoals of them,
tidily-tied, like tinned fish, resting
in adjacent pools and backwaters, unthrifty;
at loggerheads with the mainstream flow and race.
Larger boats, lesser ships, all shapes and registration.
Harbour etiquette of spinning radio-consciousness,
plimsoll paper-work, the tonnage and the tide.

Farther off, whiter-grey-whiteness of new-age windmills,
tri-winged like Dali-mutant albatross,
or some Hitchcock nightmare gull.
Slow-flapping their mesmeric energy;
here, a fine balletic pointing to the sky,
there, an agile pirouetting to the earth,
now, a slant snatch at some bird-table roof.

Next comes a variant to these odd species;
crane flamingos, all colours, except pink,
pulling up their food from boat-bellies,
disgorging on the quayside. Strangely elegant
against the vast, squat Falstaffs of crude oil.

Tall, cobalt-coloured chimneys
effortlessly blow their smoke in curves to the blending air.
Now, red bully buoys, marking unwritten lines,
shake slowly from side to side,
laughing at the indignant baritone of some hooter's blast.
As if it mattered.

Tiny dots of flotsam craft scud about,
away, beside, in front, behind,
busy as mayflies or water-boatmen.
A silent canker threatens the idlers.

Noble yachts and roughed-up hulks,
uneasy bedfellows in the common cause.

Here, flies a small and care-free, split-tailed flag;
slap-singing from a rusting house-boat mast.
This bowed pole a long-neglected waif to any paint.

And next, the warehouse labyrinths;
trapezium, round, sloped, and flat-topped acreages.
Un-ending walls signed in odd "Kr"s, "Grü"s, "Aar"s and "Oet"s.
and interminable lines of paletted "Zee"s and "Ingen"s.

Every ship declares its licensed home;
here Tobago, there Honduras, next to Bremen, then a Russian.
A thousand years of distilled trade and commerce,
Customs' men, scowls and grins, the sharp, and sleeping,
petty pilferers, and those hot embraces in the red-light nights.

And then the trade we cannot see, white cut powders, hidden
anywhere; containers, tankers, curtain-siders, swallowed condoms,
the lengths they go to thwart the sniffer-dogs!…well…

the Dutch are as laid back as their cool canals,
or so they tell me. I wouldn't know.

Everything that has passed through here has brought, and left,
its mark; ores, tobacco, wine, spinning threads, corn, coffee,
sweet-scented woods, rubber, flowers, jade, spice, engines,
and tattooed men with pythons pixelating round their arms.

Our floating palace swans disdainfully through the crowded mélange
like some high-born Duchess on her first Grand Tour;
gliding past anchors, prows and portholes, hawsers, rust and rivets,
cat's-cradle of nets, and incalculable spider-webs of wire and rope.

The counting of rich, old guilder's harvest now a hollow echo,
usurped by plastic credits, without the handshakes, or the fun.
That hallowed history has moved inexorably on,
the next phase forces through; designed, efficient, '*green*'.

The shantied sails and eager shouting stevedores
are no longer seen, or needed.

'*Buccaneers*' are just for books and poems and dreams.
Fair exchange is no robbery in this Duty-free-for-all.

But then, I am not Schengen,
and do not understand the business.

But someone ought to write about this place,
cameras have no sense of smell, unlike the dogs.

A breath of fresh air

Item: One 1930's, Napoleon-type mantel clock; stopped.
How he must have enjoyed the ticking and that sonorous gong.
He probably never even altered the hour, preferring 'old time'.
Too much trouble to add or take; better wait and tell it properly.

Item: Sideboard; wormed, minus a stamped brass handle.
He never found time to fix it, look, it's there in the drawer.
Not much trouble to put it back on, probably an antique one day.
The fruit on the stand has gone bad; we'd better throw it away.

Item: Wedding photograph in silver frame, hall-marked.
'Ida and Bill, ...St.. Steven's,..Nottingham, 19...' ,it's faded.
Worth a bit for scrap. Are you sure? I think it's E.P.N.S.
Must have been a windy day, look how her veil's blown up.

Item: Fireside chair. Is it a Parker-Knowle? Doubt it,
anyway, the arms are through, no-one recovers them today,
and besides, that's not how you spell it. No 'e', ...or is it?
After she died, they said he threw the other matching one away.

Item: Majolica jardinière; with aspidistra plant, with dust.
Needs watering. They sell them by the leaf nowadays.
God, why would anyone want a plant that has no flowers?
Faded curtains, forget them. Windows never been opened for years.

Item: Pipe rack; oak, with Minton ashtrays, one cracked, two pipes.
Filthy habit, glad it's banned, a left-over from the War.
Never did him any harm, can't have, eighty-three is not so bad.
Lucky he didn't set himself alight. Open the door for a bit will you?

Item: Old sofa; embroidered antimacassar. Cat hairs, ugh!
Smells of incontinence. Put it out for the Council to collect.
The new people will soon get it right; new brooms and all that.
Everything's going. As a house, it's not really too bad though,
'Ripe for modernisation'. All it needs is a breath of fresh air.

Helmikuu

Month of the pearl are you!
Melting snow re-gripped to inertia,
Winter taunting the foetal Spring.

Cat-like, he nearly lets you go,
retracts those icy claws just briefly,
then catches at your fluidity again
in his malevolent stasis of power.

Every twig and branch a solid waterfall,
here transparent, there opaque,
flashed in brilliant light or soft diffusion,
bodied without body, nacre of nothingness.

And after this suspended equilibrium,
this oscillating hold and release,
you finally escape, with all your skittering pearls!

Kite

Natural as air itself, the puissant Kite,
having all the parts for flight required.
An elegant raptor, though with some carrion duties,
those efficiencies of ecological recycling, politely Kite.

And cognisant - *not needing Darwin's deliberations,*
what took him so long to figure it out? – of survival.
Kite knew all about it for centuries, it wasn't hard to adapt!

Perfect design; economy on wings, and adequate armaments,
mainly reliant on thermals, - *but with one reserve engine -*
empowering those divinely simple dihedrals in glorious upflight.
Then, employing gravity - *part Stuka* - brings a diving destruction
- *landing gear supreme, so useful for those Entebbe snatches,*
grappling-hooks-to-manual - for the alive, or dead.

Vision that pierces acre on acre, - *locked-on* - vicious-hungry.
Any faraway fur or crawling thing caught in the amber
of Kite's cold eyes - *though once boiling after the 'Big Bang',*
yet having long since cooled to polished cabochons –
is held to ransom, or worse; a hung, drawn, and quartered silence.

Short neck and angled head - *of earlier Concorde?* -
together with that blueprint, snippy beak - *another copyright stolen* -
Kite is better informed – *no Ground Control radio-jamming* -
cloud-slicing, summit-joining, valley-collecting, county-scanned,
no need of schoolboy's tugging string. - *or bleeping radar help.*

Livery? Rufous - *a Red Baron, blood mixed with iron oxide fleckles* -
sanguine splashes of the slaughterman, a coat of arms to terrify
the quiverers. Under-wing-camouflage of white and grey,
insignia of black wingtips, these feathered fingers of sleek death.

And the exquisite tail! A broad-forked articulation - *Stealth secret* -
 twisting, planing to the directional, - *a hirondelle mutation* -
with the axehead of baffled air following hardly keeping up,
 - *sub-sonic* - vapourless, un-polluted,
and also becomes an ardent mating fan.

Yes, admitted, Kite has a reputation as the clean-up Commodore,
- *those mediaeval middens of London needed sorting out* –
but 'shitehawk' was such a cruel nick-name, even in Tudor-speak.

But now, thankfully, those secret cradles in Wales - *wylde playces* -
have nurtured back the numbers of Kite. And I am glad. Those
boyhood false-kites that snatched us up to dizzy heights can now
fly free, - *no more linking strings, no more manglings in tree-tops* –
no more mawkish, glass-eyed, Victorian museums of extinction.
- *careers and mortgages soon overtake and pin us down likewise* -

Every old man in his mind's eye sees himself that boy;
a vast hillside, the taunting wind, that wish to fly.
Yet down to earth drop all his leaden memories,
- *an Icarus of disappointment* - another waxen fool!
While the real Kite returns to the sizzling zeniths at his leisure,

defies the sun to scorch, contented to be baptised in fire.,
Proudly shows his scars; burnt-orange wounds of furnace flight.
And finally, - *scorning any idea of Barnes-Wallis, who's he?* -
now decides a sudden thunderbolt in auspicious, flashing stoop.
Accelerant that overtakes dull gravity's sloth – *Newton's what?* –
and some small thing becomes a victim of its own neglect.

Now perched, Kite spitefully ponders the next foray of sport.
Un-cadged, un-jessed, he oscillates between the unsuspecting morsel
and that which is already dead, though not yet in rotten putrefaction.
- *thus is called ambivalence* - An omnivore of prey; either warm
relevé freshly-plucked, or undertaking cold entrée of rigor mortis.

And so, - *Kite's evolution has been so simple* - he has his manners;
take what is your own, or clear away that which is not.
The etiquette is a matter of taste, or need, or both.

What welds his occult, fierce anatomy of fire?
Just the crimson-clotted heat of desire to exist?
Some volcanic witch-spell, surgent on his phoenix feathers?
Or a dread, apocalyptic tabard etched on the preened chain mail?

No! Just Kite, the bird, - *supreme hang-glider, no pilot's licence* -
an open sky, a gobbet and some sparse nest for continuity.
May he forever parade his delicately-practised fly-past,
and leave us earthbound and wondering.
We, in leadenness, moribund and static.

Only a Tudor oaf would call him *'shitehawk'*,
dropping his coarse wit in the gutter.

Linnaeus called him 'Falco milvus'.
- *let him try and fly that dog-latin kite!*

54

Poppies

Two seeds, both sleeping,
waiting for the Springtime rain
and swallow's return.

Twin shoots full bursting,
urgent to the colouring
and coaxing of sun.

Two in the growing,
rooted in earth's honesty,
all remembering.

Twin plants of beauty,
budding to blazing glory,
love's great finale.

Two blooms on canvas,
symbols of a long-shared life,
created with care.

Twin pressed memories,
drawn from life's stitched tapestry,
woven in the paint.

Two hearts joined as one,
beating to a single pulse,
harmony complete.

Softer than the dove,
stronger than the lion's blood,
twin poppies of love.

Utstein Kloster

A visit to Utstein Cathedral.
A day of utter stone calm.

Man was here before:
Near this place he built long stone huts with turf roofs.
But who was he? Did he have Gods? Could he speak?
or did he just tap his brother on the shoulder and gesticulate?
His rough, rude dwelling was in that time before recording.

Man was here again:
Firstly in chaos, then in calm.
After Hafrsfjord's bloody conflict, around 872 A.D., King Harald cut
his hair;
a personal denial vowed until he had knocked sense into the tribes.
His country was now united, or conquered, depending on who you
were.
He was a temporary Thor and this island was his garrison;
a royal farm, central, well-guarded, fish-plentiful.
On either side of his crude palace, no longer here, were two high
lookout hills,
like twin biceps, vertiginously balanced, flexed in permanent show.
With just enough thin soil to support the crops,
and the skins that contained the meat for the spits.
A small island ruling vast lands of mountains, snow and waterfalls.
His Gods in Valhalla smiled and waited for him.
They allowed him his great chance.

Man came here again:
Around 1260. Those pious, spartan Augustinian monks
with their long hours of prayer and longer silences.
Tonsured, slavish clerks of God; the real God.

(Harald would have turned in his grave, his hair growing again.)
This handful of learned minds knew things;
writing, translating, recording, healing, growing herbs, growing wise.
Supported by, in awe of, lesser men, those who could work;
kept in ignorance, kept for tithes, kept as children.
Keeping the monks, who didn't work, for they were too important,
or so they told their children.
These children could catch fish, slaughter sheep,
gather the berries and empty the middens.
There were also those of a fatter purse as well; a few.
They could purchase a small corner of heaven, at a reasonable price.
Those with no money just hoped and prayed for the best, or worked
harder.
All was governed by some far Cardinal's control, with some cardinal
sins.
The Kloster grew rich, relatively, land was amassed.
Two hundred and fifty souls helped it to flourish;
they kept perhaps twenty or so monks in food and fuel,
who, in turn, prayed for them and their souls. How kind of them.
It must have been useful to know that ten men worked for the upkeep
of just one monk.
Monks who intimated they were too clever to work.
But to be fair, the monks could only speak infrequently,
these monkey-businessmen were very quiet about it.
Touching another monk's shoulder to signify a desire to speak,
gain access to the Chapterhouse; to discuss....
the wages of their children? or the tithes?
or the latest reliquary, hot from Rome? Their desires?
And now, the tiny cathedral, and God, and Valhalla, is all that is left
from those earlier times,
and the echoes of chants, time-reflected candles, shadows from the
chill cloisters,
and perhaps a buried dragon-ship of Harald's, as yet undiscovered.

Man was here still later;
a reforming dissolution, in 1537, a different God came, and not of
Valhalla.
Well, the same God as before really, just in different clothes,
and eventually without the Latin, or the relics, or the flagellation.
No wonder the monks were ousted, they had out-stayed their
welcome;
roughly around the time that their children learnt the power of
knowledge.
Those children began to recognise what the system was:
a greedy, little nest of drones, silently eating their honey,
doling out penances and excommunicant fear.
Those seldom-speaking monks now spoke even less;
it's difficult when you have lost your head.
Murder always leaves one side quiet
Perhaps God didn't save them? Who knows, I don't.
Monks foully murdered; well, the Reformation was long overdue,
if a little over-zealous.
So, with no willing hands, or holy orders to obey, the Kloster
slowly crumbled.
Given over to Trond Ivorsson, now there's a name and image to
ponder on;
a local bailiff, a small God, who at least spoke Norse, and worked.
At that time even the old Abbot's House became a pigsty.
No change there then, well perhaps slightly, pigs don't bother to tap
each other on the shoulder before getting into the trough.
And at least someone cooked their bacon and emptied the middens,
cheerfully?

Man came back again, around 1700.
Hr. Christopher Garmann saw a real estate opportunity,
and developed it to his liking into a splendid country seat.
A rich Merchantman with an splendid isolationist existence idea.

A Norwegian idyll, away from 'Trade', which actually was his God.
Now, newly painted, panelled doors replaced the nailed planks,
chinoiserie furniture was the vogue, though the sheep-fat candles
stayed on.
He even had portraits done of himself and his family.
Impressive, though a shade naïf; and their noses not their best
feature!
A few struggling gravestones to them proclaim a distinct air of
importance;
though it was hardly the hub of Europe.

Man came back again.
A 20th Century rebuilding; the Kloster as phoenix.
Now bought by the Norwegian State, recognising the cultural
importance of the place,
just after the noble Schancke family had been moved on; they were
not there long.
Presumably they moved the Garmanns on? By tapping their ideas?
Or by tapping them on the shoulder, perhaps?
Who knows, they would.
Now, there was a gradual and sensitive rejuvenation of the holy
stones, in God's name.
Utstein means *'out stones'* - quarrying really. Not really an
Augustinian Latin term;
Far too sweaty, and stones won't move by themselves, however hard
you pray.
So, the Cathedral's re-incarnation came about, in keeping, though
without the relics, etc.
But with a very modern, almost alien, organ; for the recitals and the
singers.
'Gregorian chant remixed', a cover version, Godly C.D.s. even.
You may now hire the space for a Concert venue, paying a tithe to
the organisers.

'We can seat 250 here.' No real change, if you think about the monks' audience.

The magnificats and requiems are re-sung in cultural appreciation.

In Latin, of course, not Norse. We wouldn't want sheep-slaughterers and fishermen to understand.

(Valhalla still sulked, Harald's skull began to sprout again!)

As Concert-goers we can fill the place, fill the middens, both aseptically, and sceptically.

Green issues are going so well nowadays; we can now arrive at the island by tunnel.

It doesn't disturb the salmon - which are no longer there now.

The protected seals have eaten them all, so now they must farm them, the salmon that is.

Harald would have soon sorted that out, smoked seal tasted so good!

The Garmanns and the Schankes would have smiled at the Trade it now brings in,

although it does spoil the solitude somewhat,

especially all the new local oil industries, getting rid of those smelly mutton-fat candles.

How the monks would have smiled too, benignly, quietly,

tapping us on the shoulder and proffering the alms dishes; large.

Man comes here quite often nowadays;

the Kloster is a National Treasure,

a cultural gem, a museum, a splendid conference centre.

And we no longer tap our brothers on the shoulder at these meetings.

We just interrupt, how very civilised (Harald would have approved.)

And, miracle of miracles, the place is now endowed as a place for marriages.

According to God's Holy Law, not Valhalla's.

Cana! Hallelujah! Amen! the monks would have shouted, or chanted,

or rather, whispered it under their breaths, celibate in celebrant,

And now the water really is changed to wine! There is a God!

No horned helmets of foaming lager though.
But would Harald have enjoyed champagne?
The catering kitchens serve up the Wedding Breakfast in the
Refectory,
you can stay the night, book all the bedrooms. No rising for matins
though.
The few, wise virgins will tend their lamps, or mutton-fat candles,
and the many foolish virgins will burn theirs at both ends nowadays.
After matrimony comes alimony and social services for the children.
Divorce lawyers are the new Gods nowadays.
But please keep the noise down; some people are tapping other's
shoulders; the monks' ghosts are trying to listen to each other.

Man is here at Utstein Kloster for all the holiday weeks now;
which actually means all-year-round, a total lack of solitude now.
They come by luxury coach, via the tunnel, under the fjord.
Hafrsfjord tunnel, six kilometres long, perfect for a surprise attack on
Harald.
We'll cut his hair for him they say, even shave him, like a monk,
tonsured.
We'll tramp through the Kloster, plundering with our digital
cameras,
gawping at the scenery, leaving footprints on the chancel,
filling their memories, the litter baskets, the toilets,
looking at, not reading, the tombs of the Garmanns, and Schanckes,
buying the postcards and booklets, which they later forget on the
coach luggage rack.
Travel-commerce is the New God here. No merchandise from
Valhalla though.
Garmann & Schanke Tours would have done well, opening up their
stately pile.
Trond Ivorsson would have made a good guide, putting on a plastic
faux-horned helmet;

Trond, he of the long-flowing, flaxen hair, translating from the
Norse, un-cut.
Trond, he of the hefty biceps, black leathers and six-pack of lager.
So like his Great, great, great, great, great, great, ………Harald the
Hippy-haired,
Harald, the minor God, who could get very nasty if you tapped him
on the shoulder.

We were here today;
just to look, walk around, feel the peace of the place,
getting to know all the inhabitants, feeling God tapping us on the
shoulder,
whispering to us to ignore the vertiginous Odin and Thor, twin
muscles of Valhalla;
advising against becoming over-familiar with the Garmanns and
Schankes, (a plague on both their middle-class houses!)
and telling us not to tip Trond Ivorsson, because he will only spend it
on the Lottery,
and that we should become 'Patrons of the Mosterøy Organ
Concerts', or at least 'Friends',
not forgetting to sign the 'taxpayer' slip which means an extra
covenant income for them.

But, it is beautiful here;
there is a special tranquillity about the place.
Our guide told us, after tapping us gently on the shoulder,
that she brings some of her 'Patients' here occasionally.
She is part-time; they are patient. Just like the Hafrsfjord,
still and deep.
Even those who permanently rock back and forth, normally or
abnormally, go quiet here.
It is astounding, she says, they get patience, in time.
They get a wonderful sense of timelessness and peace, she says.

No change then. It all seems like it were yesterday.

It is time. We have to go.
It is time to go, we all go eventually;

I tap a stone gently on its shoulder, and whisper a question.
It answers: Yes, there is a God, though no-one has seen him.

But he is probably about to tear his hair out with all these
whisperings.

Because it was such a quiet island when he had it to himself...

  ...and there were salmon then...

    ...and an utter stone calm...

On a Cousin ill

We came to see you, long since visited.
The day was rich, time began ticking again.
We had a closer bond than most. Cousins; more,
coming from three brothers wedded to three sisters.

You sounded the same, looked older,
face fuller, and some salt in your hair.
Treatments haunted your brave eyes,
though never your smile, nor your spirit.

A worry, diagnosis, words not uttered by us,
but spoken, so out-spoken, by you.
Sounding like that determined, vigorous branch
you always were. The chance of pruning talked of.

We recollected old times; you amazed at memory,
eagerly tasting present and past harvests.
Not sap returning, not curling leaf, nor frost.
Just the best ones, this, merely an early season.

Picking ripe Victorias - more in those cycles -
the warm, corn day enjoyed again, again.
Another strike for the weighing, the perennial
brass jam pan's provision for those colder days.

Your dog, more than any staunchest friend,
licked the tears from your eyes, you said.
And those on either side of you, giver and taker,
your mother and son, your planter and plant.

Barley seas bending to the combine's will;
young heifers striding to the bankside trough;
a grandchild's blossoming cot; fruit of the season;
Nothing ever dies, continuation reigns.

Arboretum

Here I sit; stilled air, close-cut grass.
Every tree like another man, other to his neighbour.
Tall and lesser men, come to this parade-ground arboretum.
At attention, waiting for the command, all trooping the colours:

stout chestnut generals decorated with red cockades, white plumes,
laburnum brigadiers, sardonic, yellow braidings pinned,
white bracts festoon the prickly hawthorn sergeants,
sappers in camouflage; Green Howards, Green Sherwoods,
darker greens of foreign men-at-arms, needle sabres poised,
young cadets, seed pods stirring, a growing company.

Earlier, this day, we had talked of war, about war,
of polished top brass with ineffectual swagger-sticks.
We, peacefully weighing war's futility; wasted blood, the horror,
so easy in the tunes of those who never had to sing in earnest.

Here they stand; silent rooted in closed ranks,
no noise of battle or sirens blaring,
no muted orders or muffled drums.
here no sound or fury, just an ordered hush,
here the men are quiet, contemplative in nature's peace.

The only jarrings come from some high geese in the closing sky,
honking sarcasm of return to arms; a quisling, vile reveille.
Their cowardice in white feathers, a gaggling propaganda.

Here, in these woods, there is a noble resignation.
These passive trees have become a testament in green.
Earth giving sustenance to her brood of solid offspring.
These brothers and sisters guarding her soil,
her tranquility endorsed, Nature re-deployed

Now, wodwo spirits weave gently among the leaves,
a bat swoops in to sign an erratic signature to the Treaty,
thrush-plaintive comes one more sad Last Post.
Here I sit, in legacy; at peace, under these trees.

Sounds

Sounds are simply
moving invisible colours,
they feel, they touch,
transport to a different age,
a mood not experienced,
a place un-visited.

Letters and notes are just
symbols of composition;
a blue-print of another's soul.
Pictures, textures, tears;
the magic is created,
infusing minds and hearts.

An audience is needed;
space allotted, time standing still
echoing another dimension.
Each person hearing the same sounds,
their own thoughts colouring differently,
their own lives reflecting.

Creators leave a plan;
Two hands, a keyboard, a voice, a book,
the spell is woven. Performers interpret,
sounds live. Nothing is seen,
except in the mind's eye of memory
and the hearing of colours.

Skins

A snarled moon-face, sensing blood
in the instant before death, a legend
babbled from the dhobi's wild-eyed fear.
On gilded coat, coal-rich veins streaked
from drench of humidity; like viscous
honey set with burnt-black scars.
Furnaced amber retaining molten terror,
with serpentine-twitched tail, a kinetic
bristling still in the pug's light stealth.
His burning paths, alarming the peafowl's
raucous cheap enamels, still pouring
from the crucible of his mystic strength.
Eyes in fixed sun-setting glare, striations
in memory of tawny grasses, his clawed
force held tamely down on hideous rack.
Now, stretched thin, splayed, crucified
on the wax-polished floor, mirrored
in his own uniquely scored graffiti.

Also here, a currency of lights, tripod, film
camera lens and animus lust. A writhing girl
above him; some nameless, pinchbeck nude.
Feline allure; that soft-porn mockery
that blights his treasure, pampering
her pale skin with some transient fame.
Time stilted, the coarse, brief images
now smirk from some damp gutter,
while voyeurs feed off his sacred ore.
And somewhere faraway; a vacuum,
a place that longs for his pungent spirit,
and mourns his missing growl.

Flagg Races

Cluntering hooves and a twenty-mile sky
    that touches the rimming horizon of hills.
Time-honoured race by the cowshed and sty,
    with creak of the leathers and courage that thrills.
Walking the paddock and thumbing the race card,
    a nod to the neigbours while studying form.
Picking the winner; the spots? or the barred?
    a nip from the hip flask to keep yourself warm.
Appraising the silks with some knowing looks
    at the Bookie's fast-chalking to lessen the odds.
Jockeys are mounted, the hunting horn spooks,
    those cantering stilts fling such elegant clods!
Then they're off! Binoculars out of their case,
    scanning the course for the one that you've backed.
Galloping steadily, pacing the race,
    the favourite lies third, extra weight has been packed.
Out to the country, the furlongs thrumming
    now hidden by huddle of farmstead and copse.
Mad-scattering cows while flying and jumping
    with Pegasus wings and stirrups and crop.
Across the old lane, the crowd look askance,
    the winning-post beckons outsider's surprise!
A look to the rear, the chasers last chance
    to threaten the hero and snatch back the prize.
The good-natured folk cheer the winning horse,
    you picked the right one as it won by a nose.
Rosettes awarded, enclosure's applause,
    a good day this time, though it usually snows!

Pavane for Vera

Now age and care have outrun youthful times
her dance of life becomes a statelier one.
And wisdom comes when energy resigns,
no need to prove the things that she has done.

This mother, seeing children growing old,
is blessed to know her time was not in vain.
A hard life has its just reward tenfold,
as love and warmth outweigh the briefest pain.

Her strength lives on for those that wish to share,
her rules are there to bend, but never break.
Advice, when asked, is always firm, but fair,
with time to give, reluctantly to take.

Those quiet, knowing eyes now gently fade,
her measured steps of steadfastness are made.

Leafing through pages

New words of Spring come fresh, like buds,
        pushing out, youthful-green and unbruised.
Summer sings pages that rustle and shade,
        mirth and madness, fulfilled, so soon used.
Printing falls to Autumn's wet pressing,
        chapters bound up in memories' gild.
Snow-dusted shelves of wisdom and age,
        Winter well read, a library filled.

*(Please **don't** make a **gaffe** in some **mo**torway **caff**
by **ask**ing the st**aff** for neck-**end** of gi**raffe.)**

Giraffe

Oh **please**
don't **laugh** at the **tall** giraffe,
just **kind**ly **knit** him a **very** long **scarf.**
His **four** legs are **stilts,** with a **gait** that **lilts,**
And his **skin** has **shapes** like **eider**down **quilts.**
His **neck** is a **crane,** with a **hint** of **mane.**
He **claims** his do**main** on Africa's **plain**
With **two** stumpy **horns,**
and a **sneer** that **scorns,**
he **lives** on dry **leaves**
and occasional **thorns.**
He **tries** not to **sneeze**
as he **brows**es the **trees,**
and those **wa**tering-**holes**
are so **bad** for his **knees.**
With **big,** haughty **eyes**
that sug**gest** a sur**prise,**
he goes **stro**lling a**way**
on such **el**egant **thighs.**
And so **sparse** is his **tail,**
a thin **fly-**whisking **flail,**
that **some**how just **seems**
to be **quite** out of **scale.**
If you **want** any **proof**
that he's **of**ten a**loof,**
Just **don't** get too **near**
to his **rear-**kicking **hoof.**
Don't **call** him a **goat,**
and **please** never **gloat**
if gi**raffe** becomes **hoarse,**
he's a **very** sore **throat.**
He's **ra**ther quite **mard,**
and re**sents** very **hard**
if you **tell** him his **name**
was once **Camelo**pard. *

71

First Cockerel

He brazens a challenge to the new day,
then, with a bullying peck, urges his women-folk
to go forth and seek out the croft and orchard.

His tambourine wattles shake alarmingly,
as his nodding coxcomb strafes the lower
branches of the hedgerow, still dew-spelled.

Then, dancing in tight circles, he gaily struts,
spreads wide the hackles of his glossy surcoat,
and runs to the hillock's edge to view his kingdom.

Next, springs to the proud battlements of the cote,
a fancied citadel, though mere tarred felt and lath,
claps his wings and crows another proud reveille.

The yellow triangles of his spurred feet
glow richly on the black-back, sanded roof.
Down he drops, charges to the dusting-hole,

creates a mad, exotic mirage of cloud exuberance.
The dull, first-foraging bumble bees of morning
diligently scan the apple blossom in respect.

Suddenly, this gallant fowl bravely chases off
an insolent, marauding butterfly from
his rhubarb jungle in the corner of the yard.

As growing light burnishes his proud enamels,
he hops along the wall to the highest coper,
and affirms a third denial of disloyalty to the sun.

Twelve

There was once this foreign guy called Syman Piotr Cephaspetra, He came here illegally, and worked for cash on building sites. Someone joked he was the son of a Greek shipping magnate, though he denied it. Sometimes Syman smoked a bit of dope, but never touched the hard stuff. He had an ear for music and gradually built up a popular rock group. Ridiculously he called it "Pete and the Cockerels", nevertheless he had three big hits.

Then there was a man called Andy, who was a bit of a loner really. The son of a Scottish crofter, which probably explains why he was called Andrew. He was a good fisherman, though some of the locals suspected he was possibly gay. That story started when an old school friend called John once came to stay with him. John was a Baptist minister, who was later tragically killed in a terrible accident. Andy never married, and became a recluse. He never really got over losing his friend.

Next? James, nicknamed 'The Great Hulk'. A blacksmith; a real son of thunder. Mr. Strongman, all B.O. and energy. He had fists like hammers; his wife knew that. Blacksmiths sweat a lot and they drink a lot. But anvils don't bruise like a woman can. Yet James always mowed the Churchyard grass with one of his own hand-made scythes. His dad was buried there. Sometimes James would disappear behind the Church, and cry. His wife never left him; how could she? There was nowhere to go, and James needed her.

There was also his brother, John, his real job was a policeman, but he was also an occasional male stripper. Once he was drafted down to London in the middle of some riots. He enjoyed that. It gave him a chance to really get stuck in, especially on the 'darker ones' as he called them, and the extra wages came in handy. As did all the cash from those dodgy Clubs he performed in. Though at those 'Hen-Nights' there were never any women wearing burkas. John always demanded his kids behaved; he didn't want them to turn out like him.

The next was called Philip; a convicted shop-lifter. Nothing really serious, after all they make enough profits don't they? They shouldn't tempt people to steal, putting everything out on display like that. It's only natural; we've all got to eat. He was always a bit short of money for the essentials because he gambled at the bookies a bit; sometimes a lot. Philip loved the horses, but they just didn't go fast enough. Slow horses; fast women; that was him. But he always made sure his mum had enough to eat; he just passed it over.

Bartholomew! An Afro-Caribbean gospel singer. A bass voice like chocolate and a smile like a polished keyboard. He loved his purple gown and clapped his hands as all the other singers swayed and hypnotised. Testify! Testify! He took the Collection every Sunday. But why did the amount he watched put in never agree with the amount that was counted later? Bart just couldn't help it. He knew it was wrong, he knew he was a sinner. But surely God would forgive him. High five! Give the black man some skin! Hallelujah!

And next? H.M. Customs and Excise; Yours officially, Matthew; the V.A.T. man. It was a well-paid job, pension cast-iron, efficiency bonus assured. No cuts here. Render unto The Treasury that which The Treasury thinks is accountably possible. Percentage of percentage of percentage is only money after all. It doesn't hurt anyone. Poor Matthew, how can anyone like a tax-gatherer? Except those off-shore firms perhaps? He bought a pub with his redundancy money, but stayed teetotal, and always wore Levis.

Then came Tommy Didymus, a ventriloquist. The man with the alter-ego; his mirror-self. He put his hand inside a puppet and it made him feel safe. No doubt about that. He couldn't think that the twin talking to him was himself. The tragi-comedy of it all! The flamboyant costume, the thrown voice, the wooden echo, the duplicity. But it was the puppet which was real; he was the stooge, the straight man, deadpan. No-one doubted his talent, except him. Inside every clown there is a serious man trying to get out.

Ah, James. No-one knew his surname; he'd worked in the factory so long it didn't matter. "Where's James?"; "James'll do it."; "Give it James to sort out."; "Still here James?"; "You know, James…what's he called?" James just didn't know how to say "No". He was the one they all knew, but didn't know at all; a man in the shadows. He never sent, or got, any Christmas cards. No-one really knew where he lived. His dad was called Alf. Nothing more, or less, was known. He was just…James.

Now this next one is a puzzle. He had three names: Lebbaeus, Jude, Thaddaeus. A quiet sort; a scholar. He had a good heart, but never really got into the swing of things. He was shy and didn't say a lot. Someone said that he once went to a going-away party and spoke only once. His family probably came from Eastern Europe; he talked about Turkey and Armenia a lot. He was always interested in things that seemed impossible; lost causes and the underdog-syndrome and anything else obscure.

Then there was Simon. The agitator, the rebel, the one with the spray-can and the store of Molotov cocktails. His library was Marx, Trotsky, Mao, and, oddly, Hitler. He had a suspended jail sentence; he'd made death-threats to the Embryo Testing Centre. Simon absolutely honestly believed he could change the world, starting in Hackney. He lived with, and loved, a brilliant young violinist, though she was the daughter of a Duke. But he would have loved her still, even if she'd no.......well, no zeal like the converted.

Lastly, Judas; the one who worked for the Council. He was also a committed Charity worker. It appalled him that 'chavs' could spend so much money on cosmetics. Just think what he could do for the poor and the down-and-outs with that kind of money. Judas asked the Council for some support for the Community Centre where he helped out. They gave him some finances, but then they proved he had leaked some sensitive information, and pocketed some of the cash. Judas couldn't live with it. He hanged himself in the park.

Twelve men. But they all had one thing in common; they all changed after they met one particularly amazing man. None of them chose their lives. Perhaps they were chosen?

This piece of writing was inspired by a series of twelve paintings by Harold Riley, the Salford artist. They were exhibited in Manchester's Anglican Cathedral many years ago.
I have known Harold as a very dear friend for nearly 50 years.
His paintings of The twelve chosen Disciples, together with some words of poetry by the playwright, Keith Dewhurst, were considered very controversial by some people at the time that they were shown.
In my short descriptions of an alternative modern 'twelve' I have tried to incorporate some different contemporary links, along with old references, motifs, similarities, and dissimilarities; all juxtaposed to the original Disciples. My imagination ran riot in portraying them all in present day possibilities. Perhaps the explanatory notes on pages 143,144 and 145 read against the main text might help to illuminate the piece better. But I acknowledge The Bible as the authentic source for the names of the original twelve.

Love practically

The want, and the lack, and the thrill of it,
the losing, and sharing, and chill of it,
its flood, its desert, burned volcano, and balm,
and the sound, and the found, and first blush of it.
The take, and the fake, and the fill of it,
the needing, and searching, and bill of it,
its blood, its pleasure, spurned advances, and harm,
and the feel, and the seal, and first touch of it.
The gorge, and the famine, and fun of it,
the hoping, and caring, and shun of it,
its body, its shadow, learned lessons, and charm
I believe we receive if we give of it.

Skylark

What hours you fill with bursting heart of song,
your silver shrapnel spinning to the ground!
Spring-risen morn to herald, clear and long
your trembling fanfare piped in glorious sound!
What cause desires your upward flight of wings?
Ascending levels pause, each phrase renew,
then silent fall, fresh call for encore rings
to stage of boarded green and backcloth blue.
Composers, divas, choristers all try
to emulate your skill, with poor degree.
Your mordents, trills, glissandos drench the sky,
unique, inspired, your spirit filled with glee.
Why flaunt aloft, make jealous earth-bound man?
Perhaps you simply sing because you can!

Masca

The road is a serpent;
languidly strangling the mountain,
descending from the topmost view,
down and around the barren rocks,
easing around the precipices,
gripping in its black coils.
And as we travel downwards,
hanging on to the surface scales,
mesmerized by the depths,
down into that fanned chasm,
there comes a pleasing horror,
a fascination to reach Masca.

Finally, the few small casas reached;
a hamlet of splendid isolation
halfway into this vulcan valley.
Here, narrow ledges of cultivation;
deep below, through a narrow gorge,
the flashing sea, the world.
Here they came, those first men;
climbing up from small boats,
looking for a secret place,
a perch for civilisation, a home.
Four hundred years ago, they came,
they called this wilderness their own.

Those early Mascan men chose well;
a hidden refuge far from the world's trickery.
Slowly, they cut a vein of life into the barrenness,
surely, they teased sustenance for their children,
hanging on by a thread. Content with enough

and satisfied; for what more is needed.
Why would men choose here?
Attempt the impossible, and succeed?
This pass, carved through the mountain,
sculpted with ingenuity, daring to succeed,
seems almost a travesty; a trespassment;
a later insult to the stark, initial paradise.

And so we travel on, leave this place,
grabbing the second snake-road outwards,
upwards, gasping at the next far summit;
leave this odd Shangri-la of Masca,
glad and yet terrified for the coming ascent,
disbelieving our indicated exit to freedom.
And now, suddenly, I think of Laocoön;
those twin sea-snakes strangling his body,
tying his two sons to him in a rope of death.
These two mountain roads in similar fashion,
squeezing away the old civilisation,
denying the ancient, sacred solitude.

Yet still we climb, up, away from Masca;
the tale of Troy rekindles once more,
the black serpents curl round and around,
first the ankles, legs, then thighs,
rising round the hips of the mountain,
across the belly, the straining torso!
Writhing along the arms and shoulders;
up the near-vertical neck to the summit,
tight around the crown of the peak,
the cloud halo of hair is breached!
A once-Trojan village is laid bare to attack,
another mountain, like Laocoön, is conquered.

Yet, of course civilisation must move forward;
these links were inevitable, necessary.
The romance of solitude is a questionable state,
humans need humans, most of the time.
But I have a sort of revulsion against these snakes,
a kind of pity about the loss of serenity.

And as we look back down,
it is though time took us back,
back to a simpler age for a while.
A fearless, proud time of sinew and faith,
when humans could live in solitude,
when Masca's chasm was free of snakes.

Two Fires

A faint, suggestive blush on waking cloud,
like first-time glance between two lovers not
yet sure the other's thoughts are shy or proud;
that sudden spark which grows to passions hot.
New-rising Sun now chases night away,
those doubts that Moon surrounds herself, and yet
his flames will soon burn out at close of day,
as she comes back to soothe when he is set.

These to and fro demands of dark and light,
in ebb and flow, eternal balance keeps.
Like ice on fire she melts by his fierce lips,
then gratefully he cools in tears she weeps.
His bolder rays may scorch her paler light,
her gentler glow returns, and his eclipse.

Fukushima

A stricken place;
science out of control,
the latent heat building, re-building,
feeding a deadly holocaust.

Like Prometheus, chained to the rocks,
eagles from earthquakes
and giant waves from the deep
came clawing and drowning relentlessly.

Man strives bravely against these monsters;
this one, of his own making.
Nature has merely smashed the chains,
unleashing former usefulness that now threatens.

Meltdown; the hideous catastrophe looms.
Thermodynamics, plutonium, radiation;
such high-sounding knowledge, such risk.
All for the sake of a million microwaves.

And the tragedy is we are all responsible.
Natural disasters we cannot guard against.
Our own, the innocent must pay for.
Our silence on caution, our nemesis.

Pity the people, judge the plan.

Our Jack

Our Jack does goose-steps, Hitler-handed,
screams and shouts, so propaganded.
He wears a black shirt, Nazi fashion,
his uniform is Third Reich ration.

Our Jack draws swastikas a lot,
manipulates and plans and plots.
He struts his stuff in tight jackboots,
and hates all other peoples' roots.

Our Jack draws on his formal drape,
black barathea cut to shape.
He means trouble, boasts his might,
and always looking for a fight,

Jack looks down on parson's plight,
by blocking vicarage chimneys tight.
Then he fills his draughty nest,
with stolen goods, the nasty pest.

Our Jack adores his filthy stack,
and draws graffiti, whitewash flak.
He daubs bird-lime on the gable,
and splats the T.V.'s Sky dish cable,

Now our Jack's dead, his sightless eyes
no longer scan for thieving prize,
And now he's gone to sweet repose,
don't think I'll miss him, I suppose.

Our Jackdaw had an evil side,
never Jekyll, always Hyde.
Our chimney-sweep, so I've heard tell,
now grins, and hopes he rots in Hell!

Bridge

That tranquillity you saw;
leaves, grasses, a wakeful bird,
cool air lifting the darkness,
the old earth rolling, unheard.
That sweet calmness you felt;
trees, river, a new dawn,
breeze stirring the stillness,
a weight too long bourn.
That loneliness you knew;
loss, problems, illness known?
Your bridge linking two worlds:
new, unsure; past, outgrown.
And have you won your peace,
let go the harrowing strife?
Shunning this brief event,
gained a different life?
Did you know your way,
see an easy ending near?
Losing the dross and pain,
crossing the void to clear?
What's this brief span?
This anxious breath?
This easing bridge
to light, from death?
Are you at peace,
contentment found?
Come answers none;
in shrouds, no sound.
We simply ask,
shrug and sigh.
Respect choice;
we all die.

Fired Clay

Soft grey,
easy in fingers,
a specially chosen earth,
moistened, thrown, eased in form,
morphed to something
other than clay.

Drawn up,
trimmed down,
obeying the rules,
yielding to designer's studied art.
Waiting for the test of
the poisoned cup.

Moved along,
mass produced,
some commissioned,
warned threat of collapsing,
cracks in the weak, or
noble and strong.

Kiln fired,
ranked by value,
timed to perfection,
tested to ultimate end of nerves.
the best come through,
a style desired.

Ultimate heat,
fine boned, fatless,
yet still that fragility

in pitiless horrors of Hell,
an honourable service,
honed, complete.

Final release,
some pity shown,
little reward, less known.
How like fired clay is a soldier's life.
Used until broken, then stacked in
museums of peace.

First breath

She knows her time is now,
the pangs mete out her future.
Ever more those pains becoming closer,
rhythms stronger; the breathing gaps such short relief.

She knows that I watch her,
her head thrown back, panting skyward.
The pawed, rustling straw her chosen corner;
folded in these limestone walls, time-bleached beams and slate.

I know that special sound,
that hummering in her constricted throat.
A floating, enclosed bleating, stress-imbued and only
given at this time; pervading crisp, cold air of dark-before-the-dawn.

I know what I must do.
Wait, till nearly at the end,
catch, slowly turn her down and lay her fleece;
give soothing sounds, probe, and gently check that all is well.

She knows. She has been here before.
Purpose of our mutual increase and response;
linked in season's time, supporting each to the welcome.
She; source, I; helper, yet only if all thrives in Nature's living plan.

I know the easing slime, then feet, and head,
the slithering body, severance of blood, a shake.
That first, small gasp of air, vital, lest the life be stilled.
Oh, the joy of that first breath, a sneeze, a shake, and breath again,
again!

May on Dove Banks

Sweet May comes shyly to her bridal hour,
with promises of Spring fulfilled, rejoiced.
Her veils lace-drifted on the hawthorn's bower,
and music from a thousand thrushes voiced.

Where lilies-of-the-valley greet the sun,
her beauty's shadow marks where she has stept.
The hare leaps joyously where she has run,
and silver'd trout lie still where she has wept.

In fragrance stirred by pollen-heavy bees,
she waits beneath the blossom's fountainhead.
Then lightly treads through wood anemones,
young fleeces and cloud canopy her bed.

All life she loves and proves her time well spent,
these limestone banks her paradise intent.

"The Glevum Economy"

Already older than my Grandfather;
this fine piece of quaint farmyardery,
made from mahogany. Solid, like him.
Created from fine-grained, red-brown timber,
(more suited to a cabinet-maker's art)
brass-hinged and with some delicate strips of glass.
An incubator (I loved to say the word),
patented: *"The Glevum Economy"* .
With trays of meshed wire, felt-cushioned,
and a paraffin burner that was the artificial hen...

          and the turning...

That all-important job,
my first chore after school.
A commitment, no, an all-important duty.
My tiresome laces swapped for wellingtons,
the ridiculous peaked school cap, missing its top button,
discarded for the woollen, favourite one...

          and the turning...

On the front of that...
machine? apparatus? implement?
what can you really call it, a mechanical mother?
Incubator must suffice. And on the front of that incubator,
a label; a swelled, stamped-brass oval; a guarantee of quality.
Shown proudly at many a Victorian Farming Trade Fair:
'A scientific, economic wonder in the art of poultry breeding;
.unparalleled excellence in operation, vital for agricultural success'
Festooned with silver medals, painted endorsements
and ostentatious seals of approval - patents pending -
like bizarre Music Hall embellishments...

          and the turning...

It is an agrarian novelty, a mildly pro-Darwinian intervention.
Four turned legs lathed finely, thinnest boarding,
a chimney, and dampers.
More a piece of pretentious furniture than a simple tool,
proud in its own importance,
and like some fine artisan's off-cut creation,
"..don't waste that wood!"
that old fashioned thrift and rectitude…

                        and the turning…

Those cherished eggs, so carefully collected,
taken to the cellar, laid on great, crazed, blue-and-white
meat plates from old Staffordshire kilns.
Drifted on a thin layer of gingery, tobacco-coloured bran.
Each pointed sphere lightly pencilled with opposite nought and cross.
Suspended animation of two weeks, no more.
Each egg touching its neighbour in the curved clutch,
and with not one angle to spoil the symmetry…

                        and the turning…

Twice a day, early morning and evening.
revolving the, as yet, cool shells, over and over and over,
gently altering their hidden yolks to stop them dying.
The noughts becoming crosses, and turned over again, the next day.
Aping the stirring of the laying hen till she has enough to sit.
Rather, till we had enough for a brooding...

                        and the turning…

Now, inside, these rows of precious fragility
lie waiting for my hands to coax and coddle.
I swivel the half-mooned metal catches and lower the door,
slide out the tray of sleeping shells, looking like gigantic ant larvae,
and begin the ritual revolutions, a plane of life beneath my fingers.
A reverence of avian movements; my responsibility.
My fingers substituting the shuffling feathers and claws,
a jealously-guarded private stewardship and trust.

Checking the temperature, the dampers,
the sliding thermometer at its vital 103 degrees.
Watching over the glimmering life,
a gentle effleurage of tending…

                                     and the turning…

Until that anxious day,
a promise hardly dared hoped for,
those midget balls of sunshine! Cheeping in earnest!

But sadly, also the occasional demmick,
the one with the splayed legs.
And the one or two that couldn't quite break out,
the ones you cannot help, the ones that turn away from life.
and, just like the incubator, cool in memory…

Moved on to a brooder, this yellow pool of tiny birdlets
squeezes in and out amongst an eiderdown of warm air.
Above them, the infra-red lamp unblinking,
a halo to their quivering gold.
Living bits of spun-lemon-peel-candy-floss,
punctuated by scatterings of currant-eyes,
their beaks like sawdust specks.
The brittle matchstick legs go tottering
to and from the shallow troughs of mash
and galvanised drinking fountains,
They are as busy as life can be.

And my hatching duty is done.
What a fine job we did…
"The Glevum Economy"…

                   and me…

                            and the turning…

Wolf

Snow-spawned, frost-reared,
    shadow-slipping the gaunt pine bars.
Loping paws unstoppable
    in the blue wind's sifting,
        drifting over the spoor.
Glare-fixed, legend-feared,
    pity-scorning the slower kind.
Ancient code unbreakable
    in the eye's steel showing,
        glowing like molten stones.

Light-leaped, keen-eared,
    hunger-catching the scent of fear.
Glacier-grip unmeltable,
    in the pack-ice crushing,
        rushing the finished prey.
Teeth-snarled, sky-cloaked,
    out-numbering some feeble hope.
growling jaws unlockable
    in the fresh kill's gripping,
        dripping slowly the gore.

Sharp-nosed, night-sleeked,
    ghost-forming by hard, cold stars.
Howling throat unchokable
    in the mad moon's staring,
        baring open the bones.
Foul-trapped, torture-racked,
    fool-testing the baited lure.
Escape impossible in rifle sight's cringing,
        bringing the pelt of grey.

Villanelle to Salvador Dali

Persistent memory and wakeful sleep
as time plays tricks, and timeless sand then sinks
by turn of the tide in the day-night deep.

Where softened watches with melting hands keep
the meaning of dreams; oblivion links
persistent memory and wakeful sleep.

At the far off bay by the rocks' hard steep
where an un-risen moon and sunlight drinks
by turn of the tide in the day-night deep.

Remembering times of the past now seep
through an hour-glass, soft-running sand now links
persistent memory and wakeful sleep.

A thin, cankered olive bough seems to weep,
and a washed-up foetus in madness blinks
by turn of the tide in the day-night deep.

Now crawling insects in death's grim time reap
those minutes and hours, day-dreaming links
persistent memory and wakeful sleep
by turn of the tide in the day-night deep.

The Buxton YFC

Our glorious land with none compares, on this we all agree,
Custodianship of countryside begins with YFC.
Our parents, and their parents, knew to hand the future on
to children, who, in turn, would farm their land when they were gone.

These hills and dales of pleasant green that feed us as we toil,
a bounteous, fertile heritage is garnered from it's soil.
The Springtime plough, the harvest hymn, the horse and milking cow,
the fleece, the feathers, roasted beef, and pork from suckling sow.

The vegetables, the threshing floor, the orchard's fruit so sweet,
the lark's delight, the smell of hay, the barley and the wheat.
The honey's swarm, gold Autumn's hue, the stars and morning dew,
these sights round Buxton all abound, and cared for by the few.

Those ancient men that farmed the land full realized its worth,
they chose, then paired, and bred their stock, and tilled the honest earth.
God's creatures Noah counted in, by twos, then went to sea,
but Noah's maths were slightly wrong, for one and one make three!

It's just the same in YFC when courting comes about,
sons seek wives from neighbour's girls, their parents frown and doubt.
The old ones hide their memories, their own youth they forget,
yet give them all a second chance, they'd nod their heads, you bet!

And so the young ones come each week to meet at YFC,
new generations learn the craft, good farmers how to be.
The girls discuss their handicrafts, and how to be demure,
The lads learn how to judge a cow, and when to spread manure.

Debating, entertainments, quizzes, how to act on stages,
they travel over all the land, with barely any wages.
They do it 'cause they're made that way, their lot they wouldn't swap.
They smile and sing from dawn to dusk and dance until they drop.

The YFC is fun to do; the members keen to go,
the subs are very reasonable, through sunshine and through snow.
Some girls delight in Cookery, the boys can judge their buns,
And girls can learn of Safety First, while lads inspect their guns..

Be serious now! Young Farmers are the cream of all the crop,
They grow the food we need, in supermarkets or Farm Shop.
Let DEFRA go and hang themselves, for they are blind to see
the backbone of this country is the strength in YFC!

North Sea

There!
      Land!
            How far off?

Difficult for a regular earth-dweller to contemplate.
      Just a dark, grey hump with a ridge, a dorsal?
           Some whale-island, some child of Norway?

Only moments before, nothing. A cool morning
      and twin elements of fathomless sky, incalculable sea.
          Air, Water...now here's Earth,
            or rather some inhospitableness afloat.

And next comes the fourth element......Fire!......
    A tiny flash of white light, flickering,
        but, on observation, too regular to be the wild one.

A man-made regularity of pulse.........*short*...*short*.........*long*.........

Turns red, then green and back to red, then white again,
    a scant rainbow between the source and eyes.

The rhythm ritualizes again.........*short*...*short*.........*long*..........

A signal to the captain's study, some guiding buoy.
    The sea is an eerie, total calm, no wind,
        just the drowned earth rolling beneath us.

This fire language explains again.........*short*...*short*.........*long*.........
    Whatever it may mean.

To me, it seems to signify echoes of ancient times,
    a song of *oars,* growled *oaths,* and a surging *dragon head*

    ...*swing*...*drop*.........*pull*.........

    ...*swing*...*drop*.........*pull*.........

More humps...
        more whale islands...
                more swimming land....

My feet begin to itch...
        and give thanks.........

Peaklanders

We have lived here long; before and since the togas left,
scratched our earth and been grateful for the harvest.

We have kept our sheep and worn their coats, and fed,
lived in plague and plenty, seen times both rich and harsh.

We have hewn our trees, planted, made our walls, and roofed
our houses, small and great, and some of those for blessed God.

We have dressed our wells, dammed our streams and drunk,
fished, and floated in and out the goods we made or needed.

We have built our mills and factories, used our talents well,
dug our mines and quarries, laboured hard and traded wise.

We have carved our roads and bridges, brought in heat and light,
recorded, both in words and art, and kept our customs well alive.

We have helped our friends and neighbours, yet fought with some,
even sent our folk across the seas and often brought back less.

We have made our songs and dances, played our sports and games,
walked our hills and dales for no real purpose, other than delight.

We have gone away, sometimes never to return, yet accept those
that wish to share our space and kindly warm them at our hearths.

We are custodians of our land, thankful for our parent's guidance,
knowing we must pass it on again to all of those that follow after.

And although we no longer have the Paradise that Adam knew,
we are content, and welcome Lambeth here today, and all of you.

Youth by Age

Who are these arrogant youths
who clutter up the park railings?
Who are these feral yobs that sneer and spit,
swear and jostle shoppers in the street?
                    " I don't know what the world's coming to!"
These twelve-year-olds with sparkling nose studs,
who think they're nineteen, know all the world,
and laugh too loudly at each other's jokes.
                    "Never in my day, my mother would have..."
These thirteens, fourteens, smoking on the benches,
another pair spit-swapping, slightly farther off
the hooded others wishing that they were.
                    "They should bring back National Service!"
These fifteens that have all tried sex, some successfully.
Procreation's just a Government statistic, with a pram.
                    "...or at least the cane, or birch! ..."
And buzzing round the gang even younger ones,
hair gel-raised and chewing gum, or worse,
with skateboard tricks, and attitude, and bravado.
Dying for, yet unsure of, that growing hair, and proof.

Well...these young, excited, confused, neglected,
affected, scrawny, spotty, not-too-clean young... yobs...
just might be the scientists, drivers, teachers, nurses,
gardeners, surgeons, welders, beauticians, engineers,
traffic wardens, cleaners, soldiers, criminals, and M.P.s...
        that we all became...
if we give them understanding, direction, and trust.

Give thanks, and be aware...we brought them up.
just like our parents did...and look what a fine job they did?

Come March

Come and blow away the Winter,
sweep the snow-bones from the walls!
Cause the frozen lake to splinter,
wake and tune the sweet bird-calls!
Come and ease the stiffened hedgerows,
spread the coltsfoot down the lane!
Come and lighten sullen shadows,
blow the fires of Spring again!

Come and bring a warming season,
tease the sleeping buds to burst!
Bring us hope and give a reason,
watch to see which swallow's first!
Come and lengthen short, dark hours,
bring wick lambs and sweet, frim grass!
Banish ice, bring gentler showers,
let each lover meet his lass!

Come and hitch the plough and harrow,
dry the weary, sodden land!
March, in music's breeze and bellow,
come and blow your boisterous band!
Bring the Spring we always long for,
banish all old Winter's sham!
Come and sing your concert encore,
in like lion, out like lamb!

The Colonel

The Colonel had a problem, his feet were rather sore,
his toes were red and angry, which really was a bore.
His wife, the dear Clarissa, inspected them one night.
But as she pulled his brogues off, she got an awful fright.

"Good God!" she said "they're looking grim; both are just the same."
"They're purple, swelled, and scaly, I'm not surprised you're lame!"
The Colonel grunted, scowled and said, "I'm not a horse you know."
"Is it shootin'? fishin'? golf? or what? for I can hardly go."

His dear Clarissa answered him, "To my mind there's no doubt;
Glenfiddich, or Glenmorangie, has given you the gout!"
"Gout!" roared back the Colonel, "you must be ravin' mad!
for I've been drinkin' Scottish Malts since I stopped being a lad!"

"You know best," Clarissa sighed, "but looking at your feet,"
"I doubt you'll live to drink much more, do I get the country seat?"
The Colonel shot his eyebrows up, and dropped his manly jaw."
"Clarissa, dear, please don't say that, for I'll not leave you poor,"

"You'll get 'The Towers', car and yacht, cheque-book, guns and moor."
"But I hadn't planned to go just yet, d'ye think there is no cure?"
"Oh, I'll take you to the Doctor's," his dear Clarissa muttered,
"there might be treatment, pills or cream." The Colonel only spluttered.

Next morning after breakfast, James, the chauffeur, waited near.
The Bentley gleamed, their pride and joy; a classic, vintage year.
So through the Shires they grandly went to London's Harley Street.
The Colonel dreading whiskey's ban (if that might cure his feet.)

His socks were slowly taken off, a painful process that,
The doctor, St.John-Cholmondley, said "They're scaly, red and fat!"
"Well, Colonel, I'm so sad to say there really is no doubt,"
"I'll bet you twice my normal fee you've got a case of gout!"

"Will I live?" the Colonel asked "Why yes!" said St.John-Cholmondley,
"Keep off the malts; you'll live for years, no need to look so glumly."
At this the dear Clarissa smiled, for she didn't wish him dead,
but all the same she wondered just when his Last Will might be read.

James, the chauffeur, drove them back, '*The Towers*' came in view.
And at the door the Colonel said, "I know what I must do."
"I cannot bear to leave you, dear, you are my guiding star,"
"I'll change my drinking habits! James, don't forget to wash the car."

The dear Clarissa took him in, then smiled and sat him down.
"I'll send for tea and biscuits now," which made the Colonel frown.
"That isn't really what I meant, for tea's what Parsons drink,"
"and biscuits should be fed to dogs, so I'll tell you what I think."

"Glenfiddich and Glenmorangie, Glengoyne and Miltonduff,"
"Laphroaig, Inchgower and Aberlour, of these, I've had enough."
"Glentauchers and Glenrothes, Aberfeldy and Tamdhu,"
"Glenkinchie, Cragganmore, Dufftown, I'll abstain from, just for you."

"And though it's been my downfall, my one and only vice,
"I realize my feet and toes have paid a heavy price."
"I'll give up drinking malts, for St.John-Cholmondley says I ought".
"I'll cure this blasted case of gout; I'll get a case of port!"

pronounced "Singeon-Chumley"

Elephant

Only her eye is alive.
Only her eye twinkles darkly,
at centre of some ancient storm.

An eye which looks at me, I think,
with bored quizzicality of watch.
An eye so very unimpressed
with what it looks on now,
having looked down those other years,
in their thousands, in her blood.

She is a huge, strange, washed-up rock
on the beached floor of her life.
Her ears flap slowly, and again,
as there is nothing else to do.
And a tree-girthed leg is shifted,
then re-planted softly nearer,
taking wrinkled root again.
And her eye is moist with rheum.

The trunk uncurls and floats its tip
over the grim flatness of enclosure;
smells of the veldt unfound.
And the grey, dry-lichening of hide
is alien in this outrageous prison;
yet her eye seems unconcerned.

Her food is dutifully served;
the net with its captive hay
hangs in a tasteless gloom.

She was bred in this hideous place,
so far from rains and drought,
saved for the future, trophy-shielded.

The tusks are short, managed, sawn
for safety, now who knows where?
And is the lion's mane clipped?
Are the crocodile's teeth drawn?

These bars contain her massiveness,
a solitary purdah to any rampaging musth,
but her eye is free, I think.

She stands in a sleep-walked meditation.
and only her eye is alive.

Only her eye floods darkly,
the rest is a burned-out storm.

Be still

Sometimes, when I am still;
I look at things in my mind's eye,
I look at paintings in my memory,
those scenes and times of my life:
bright dawns of yellow Spring,
long days in Summer's openness,
cool afternoons in Autumn bronze
and nights of locked-down Winter.

Sometimes, when I am still;
I ponder on my life and work;
those good and not so good days.
I see old grey walls and narrow lanes,
encircling the smell of new-mown grass.
Above, cathedral skies with rising larks,
barns of sweating hay, sharp dusty stubble,
far blue hills that feed a thousand sheep.

Sometimes, when I am still;
I imagine those remembered sounds.
I hear them replaying in my memory
the bark of a fox, the sudden ploop of a trout;
geese overhead on some misty grey morning,
crows and gulls that squabble behind the plough,
an anxious sow fretting about her wriggling piglets;
and that sound that can only be the yard gate closing.

Sometimes, when I am still;
I hear the chatter and gossip of the market;
I watch the opening and shutting cattle-wagon doors,
see the slap of tar-stick and ticket on the cattle's rump,

the thwack of the gavel, then heading for home,
sometimes pleased, sometimes disappointed,
but knowing I'll come again next week,
because that's what we do.

Sometimes, when I am still;
I think of many a Harvest Festival,
of village school and carolling.
YFC, NFU or Parish Council.
Recall so much confetti in the churchyard,
sad wreaths and hope of christening gowns.
Friends met up for Whist Drives, or a drink
at The Wakes, or simply passing through.

Sometimes, when I am still;
I see so much that's changed, and yet so little.
The people merely drive a faster horse and light electric candles.
They talk to faces that they cannot see by mobile phones,
see faces that they cannot touch by Skype, yet still pay taxes.
We fly to foreign parts, down-load a thousand tunes,
can never watch all the T.V. channels that are available,
complain about our income, yet still watch for swallows each Spring.

Sometimes, when I am still;
I look into my past and try to plan my future;
even if it doesn't happen, I must still prepare.
The remembrances in my heart, the foundation of my past,
are the building blocks of experience for tomorrow.
So, occasionally in the still of night, in the still of the day;
that pause before the dawn, or in the approaching dusk,
these are all good times to be still, and even change.
For the seasons will still come; they must.
People will still grow old, children still move on,

pulling up their roots and setting down elsewhere.
For when the air is still, even when there is no wind to sail,
you can always fill the time and write new maps and charts;
plan a fresh or different voyage, a different place.
We can so often row in the wrong direction.
So be still and take a breath, ready for the next tide.

Sometimes when I am still;
yes, when everything is so still;
I think about those times when
things might have been done differently,
but hindsight is such a useless tool,
and the next day is different anyway,
but it is good to reflect, and be still for a change.
So often we are busy with the wrong things.

Be still, reflect, take stock, and pause.
But not for too long, for life is passing quickly.
Be still occasionally; think how you can improve,
think how you can make life better for others.
Be still, then let the pause of Winter's reflection
become the promise and hope of Spring.
Be still, be thankful for what you have.
Then, gather up your strength and live the day.

Stoop

Measuring the moorland tracks, it stands alone;
remote, aloof, contented to be going nowhere;
this leaning stoop gives names and miles in stone,
a linearity exact between the points that share.

In broader view, far changeless hills, those
blue horizons coming closer, marching on,
this ancient marker greets the stranger, knows
the regulars, bids a sad farewell, and hinders non.

Unperturbed by sun, new moon or evening dew,
shrugging off the fog, oblivious in the gale,
this pillar watches all those passing through
its boundary, impetus to weary feet about to fail.

Its arrows never fly, the words are dumb,
the numbers never alter, time looks kindly on
this stoic pointer, giving heart to all that come
and go, linking to some future all that's gone.

Monks and squires, highwaymen and pedlars,
hooves and wheels, merchant sales and purchase,
this silent watcher counts the barrels, medlars,
bolts of cloth, lead ingots, all in passing circus.

Poachers, shepherds, painters, mountain bikers,
those that shoot and those that watch the birds,
this milestone for the cameras of intrepid hikers
stands alone, a muse for poets scribbling their words.

The old stoop hears not, speaks not, when in question
keeps self-righteous silence under perching claw,
this rock is steadfast, ignoring rude suggestion
that, as the crow flies, distances can be unsure.

Sweet Fruit

Eve was the first to succumb to him,
      the slender, sinuousness of his movements,
luxuriating in that Paradise so soon denied.

Fascinating her in his writhing coils,
      wrapped around the sacred Tree of Life,
forbidden fruit shining, well within her reach.

For he tempted her, and she agreed,
      stroking his scales in her gratitude,
his bright skin smooth and so muscular.

For he knew, that snake, what he had done,
      and now she knew, tasting what he offered,
taking on that power with a relished laugh.

And his flickering tongue still whispers,
      cajoling, mesmerizing, sensing his prey,
she still listens; each new Eve gains her knowledge.

For should she not? Where ignorance is bliss
      the un-initiated, the pure, can blindly rejoice.
But the knowing is subtle and sublime.

Her years move on in endless rings,
      and he still moves, ever-shedding skins,
finger-marked, sloughed and second-hand.

Was Adam cuckolded by a snake?
      No, his knowledge just came hand-me-down.
But the apple still sticks in his throat.

Sounds and Senses

A cockerel wakens the dawn on feathered spur,
      hedge-rustling grass now hides some scampering fur.
Whistle and whoosh from a steaming bygone train,
      the scratch and scutter of vermin deep in a drain.
Some blacksmith honing a scythe for harvest sheaves,
      worn shuttles that go click-clack as the textile weaves.
A ploop from fly-hungry trout on the stillest day,
      with sweet lullaby of bees in mad-blossoming May.

Crackle and booming of thunderclouds angry rage,
      the feel of leather-bound books and soft vellum page.
The snapping of gorse on a spiky headland heath,
      a crunching of boots with the frosted holly wreath.
Skylight's armour fending off the hammering rain,
      an oak, dropping acorns, plans for the carpenter's plane.
Salt-creak of old hemp that tackles the mizzen spar,
      rich smell of warm spices that travelled from Zanzibar.

The tap and cheep from an eggshell's struggling chick,
      the warm, wet surprise of a faithful spaniel's lick.
The pop of a cork and tickling bubbles in wine,
      or clang of the bars, on bread-and-water to dine.
Cool, chuckling stream and pungent pine and spruce,
      the thwack of racquet, a grunt and the call of deuce.
Taste of mouthwash, a needle and mind-numbing drill,
      a coconut doze that ends with mosquito's fill.

Loud ringing that heralds a thump to the boxer's nose,
      a new pair of shoes that rub the ends of your toes.
The strict-marching beat of aging Grandfather clocks,
      strong odours that usually link to football socks.

A quarrelsome chorus of gulls behind Spring ploughs,
  the honking geese on the Nile and breeze-riffled dhows.
The troubled cry from a baby's wool-crocheted cot,
  a missed opportunity stopped by the gavel's lot.

Sweet-scented roses hidden by Tudor brick wall,
  a smoothing of velvet worn for the Charity Ball.
A roar of engines gathering speed for the flight,
  the silence of snow that blesses the land with white.
Fat, sugar-sapped buds that give birth to laughing leaves,
  as nesting swallows twitter in sun-warmed eaves
Foul-choking smoke and howling wind in the flue,
  the tender touch of one sharing life with you.

Ploughing the end of the line

Sunday morning conversations are so good:
the showing; the reading; the commentary;
the verbal editing; the pencilled notes;
the ideas; the explanation; the argument;
     the end of the line.

A pair of horses hitched to the same plough:
the younger stumbling on fresh, new ground;
the older experienced in the deeper loams;
the weather of words; the drought;
     the worry of weeds.

A preparation for Spring's hope:
the ploughing that wasn't always quite straight;
the carting off of the turned-up stones;
the harrowing in of the awkward clods;
the sowing of the new seed;
                              the rolling of rough to smooth.

An awakening of the senses to germinate:
feeling the sun talking to the tilth;
seeing the sprouting of new growth;
listening to the gentle rain of encouragement;
noticing colours warming to the ripening;
deciding the time to pick up the scythe;
                              the sharpening of the edge.

A culmination of the season's effort:
the cutting of crop: the threshing of sheaves;
the winnowing of chaff from the grain;
                              bagging the small, ripe seed.

Our shared interest is like the harvest:
the agony of the grinding quern;
the sifting of flour to fineness;
the kneading of pliant dough;
the baking of a good loaf;
                              the sharing of bread.

Yes, Sunday mornings are for sharing and over-done toast;
both so much more fulfilling than ploughing the end of the
                                                    line.

Sire

His body; bravado, a bulwark.
His forehead; some curling, mop-hair carpet.
Broadest muzzle of pink and speckled flesh, and
redolent of cool, dead turkey skin,
bled and freshly plucked. Light within
his bulging eyes; a bluish-brown, aggressioned.
Nostrils snorting power and hot, raw threat,
colossal swaggering in his sumo-walk.

He plays so easily with that massive iron gate,
horns thud-rattling in a rhythmic push.
Long-stringed saliva stretching down to
pit-prop legs, running over plate-score
splitting hooves to the ridged-out concrete floor.
Buzz-mithered hide; his thick, clarted tail conducts to
the pizzicato of flies. The mating-crush
awaits the inevitable; his brute, tumescent state.

A thunderous beldering splits the prisoned air,
his belly arches in the promised surge,
testes tighten in narcissistic pose of masculinity.
He turns and disappears inside his inner lair,
a shelter from the rain and snow, where
no door, the coldness is conducive to virility.
The scent of heifer in her heat, his spur,
he swivels on his clays and re-appears to stare.

So this, his kingdom, a courting-pit for patrons.
The foddering-hole shut off by warped and riven
oak, cautiously opened and so quickly closed.
He lifts his copper ring towards the sky

in proud display. His harem changing by
their moons, (he snuffs and curls that punk-nosed
marriage band which never can be given),
each fresh maiden batch, or those outgoing matrons.

And here, indeed, she trots, eager and sweating,
no buttercups in her hair, no fashion of rosette,
no allure or chaste promises, just the heat.
The pure, brief, animal bloat to mate.
A seasoned smell the species have to sate,
that needs no science for its simple feat.
No teasing, no encouragement, no coquette.
Disregard to human sniggers at their coupling.

Again, those battering-ram horn spars
thwack painlessly against the sullen penning.
He knows this routine which always ends the same:
the clack of certain door, some heifer quickens
pace; the dividing gate opens. His lance thickens,
her coarse feint of denial, then a blatant lack of shame.
Her fecundity balanced in the gathering,
a grunted lurch, and both seize in their stars.

And with their noble spate, no romance here,
a planned and calculated business plan.
She, content, if not exhilarated, is noted
down, a date and number on a breeding board.
Then stands in trembling shock, and un-adored.
While Sir, furious at been forced away, demoted
back to his solitary cell by some mere man,
But why so soon his conquests disappear?

But disappear they do, back to the placid fields,
the shortest of trysts, and he is once again alone.
His blazed eyes roll backwards in thwarted rage,
his shoulders risen to a gladiator stance,
grinds against the stubborn bars, he pants
and bellows, again is at the ready stage,
haunches firm, his swelling pizzle grown
to braggart championing for any that so yields.

We leave him to his futile, crazed repression,
discuss the merits of his future stock. And yet
the practiced eye of husbandry can get it wrong,
science and genetics are merely still but tools,
Nature has the last laugh and slyly overrules.
Some sires live too short and some too long,
some breed true and others breed regret.
All in all a gamble; compatible or rank regression.

For I am proud of him, yet also sorry,
the wisdom of why? how much? when bought?
Impatient for his calves to come along,
a progeny too soon too close. Eventually, I know
that one day he will simply have to go.
What the future holds? Before so very long
I will slap his rump on leaving, my throat caught,
as he goes off for slaughter in some dingy cattle lorry.

In a garden

Please, God, let me die in a garden,
on my own, in a chair, in the shade.
but not yet, though asking your pardon,
for you choose when to take what you made.
If you please, all I ask is to hear
some sweet birds, see trees, smell flowers,
feel the sun, a slight breeze, taste no fear,
know some peace in the last of my hours.
Those I love, let them find me asleep,
with a smile and closed eyes, without breath.
Let them pause for a moment and weep,
dry their eyes, knowing I've conquered death.

You've shown me the world and its treasures,
let me share in my family's love.
I have tried to give back some measure
in these lines, some below, some above.
You always remembered to wake me,
you filled most of my days with such fun.
and you never forgot to send me
to my bed, when the day was all done.
You gave me my talents, some wasted,
some blossomed; I was glad about those.
Though some words unwritten, untasted,
could be better than those that I chose.

You opened my eyes from my first day;
I was blessed with some chances to fill.
You'll close down my eyes on my last day,
let the earth have my dust, if you will.

So, please, when my arteries harden,
or a stroke, or Alzheimer's takes hold,
I'd like to expire in a garden,
don't forget, God, now you've been told.
For you gave me my life and my living,
but sometimes it seems rather odd
why you do all this taking and giving,
but I guess you know best. Thank you, God.

Christmas Rules, OK?

A season of joy and goodwill to all.
A time for greeting and forgiving all.
To think of others and serve with gladness.
To make the peace and stop the madness.

A reason to give, receive, with thanks.
A time to reflect and fill in the blanks.
To lighten your load and cast off cares.
To offer your hand and take of theirs.

A chance to redeem and start again,
A kindly deed and a comfort to pain.
To acknowledge faults and turn to praise.
To ask, and reply, and no anger raise.

A hope in all and support to the weak,
A sharing of work and cherish the meek.
To rise to a challenge, defer to what's right,
To expect no reward, defend, but not fight.

A simple life and an honest purse.
A balance to Nature, smile and not curse.
To turn the world with a single thought;
To live and love, for our time is short.

A time to listen, and not judge the rest.
A tolerant voice, encourage what's best.
To open your heart and avoid all sin.
To welcome the day and let happiness in.

A time for honour and humbled pride.
Accepting neighbour, and none denied.
To bring compassion, yet not deny mirth.
The wonder, at Christmas, of one child's birth.

To: Janus@godsrus.com

Two faces you have,
one backwards, one to the front;
the past, the future.

Two viewpoints you have,
one wrinkled, one to the dawn;
the dead, and the quick.

The Romans shut your
temple doors only four times in
seven hundred years.

At the shutting out,
soldiers diced; peace hung like mist;
weapons sighed in rust.

At your open doors
rage flew, war rode out and on,
blood boiled in the veins.

Look again, Janus;
look back over your shoulder,
do your double-take.

Why not start again?
A New Year's resolution -
bring it on Janus!

Bring another year,
but stop wars; give us some peace.
Can't you see both sides?

Or buy a mirror,
and look at yourself for once.
Even you can change.

Send me an email,
or better still, use Facebook;
or why not Skype me?

Make a wish, Janus!
What's past is past, go for it!
Don't be an anus!

Requiem

...Introit...
those faint sounds,
a stumbling onto the birthing-nest,
warm haven inbetween the barn wall and bales,
straightaway his decision: too many,
already the numbers cannot match the need,
...Et tibi reddetur votum...
the unwritten law is known, unpalatable, but strict,
the boy knows what must be done,
...Requiem aeternam dona eis Domine...
the rule; opened eyes, let live,
un-opened eyes, the die is cast,
...Et lux perpetua luceat eis...
besides, too many spread disease,
...Ad te omnis caro veniet...
the mewling kittens are gathered in his hat,
the foddergang his, and their, processional,
...Kyrie eleison...
...Christe eleison...
mercy and might unevenly dealt.
...Domine Jesu Christe, Rex gloriae...
his Sunday School prize forgotten,
the boy becomes a man,
...Libera eas de ore leonis...
his young mouth is set and clamped
to stop the quivering,
...Ne cadant in obscurum...
the coming darkness, his conscience,
...Hostias et preces tibi, Domine, laudis offerimus...

the sacrificial buckets beckon,
both half-filled with unholy water,
...*Tu suscipe pro animabus illis*...
he still remembers it to this day,
those extremes of warmth and chill,
...*Faceas, Domine, de morte transire ad vitam*...
he has seen death and life so many times already,
this time, it is his to control,
...*Sanctus, Sanctus, Sanctus*...
quickly, he throws them in,
and covers the baptism,
...*Benedictus qui venit in nomine Domini*...
closes his mind and hopes they let go quickly,
now he turns to wait in abject misery,
...*Pie Jesu Domine, dona eis requiem*…
...*Dona eis requiem sempiturnam*...
his washed hands, like Pilate's,
will never be clean again,
...*Agnus Dei, qui tollis peccata mundi*...
who will take away this sin?
what rest for him?
...*Dona eis requiem*...
...*Lux aeternam luceat eis, Domine*...
their light has been put out,
a light that had not even been seen,
...*Et lux perpetua luceat eis*...
in time, he lifts the upper bucket
and sees the stillness, the bloat.
...*Requiem aeternam dona eis, Domine*...

the waters have washed the un-opened eyes,
a little milk of kindness spills from the mouths,
and clouds the water,
...Cum sanctis tuis in aeternam quai pius es...
his un-manly tears fall down his cheeks,
their release is not enough,
...Libera me de morte aeternam in die illa tremenda...
he struggles at the death,
shakes in grief, involuntary, to his core,
...Tremens factus sum ego, et timeo...
and he is made to tremble for his manly duty,
his day so terrible, he hides in shame,
...Dies illa, dies irae...
...Calamitatis et miseriae, dies magna et amara valde...
this test, so vile, is over,
he is denied his judgement till a later day,
...Dum veneris iudicare saeculum per ignem...
...In paradisum deducant te Angeli...
he thinks of heaven, and wonders.
takes the lower bucket and his father's spade,
...In tuo adventu suscipiant te Martyres...
the grave is dug, and filled, he cannot help but think
their deaths are as nothing compared to his martyrdom,
...Chorus Angelorum te suscipiant...
this day the boy will remember all his life,
from time to time...and now.
...Aeternam habeas requiem...
...Requiem...
...Requiem.

Plique-à-jour

The snail moved imperceptibly over the glass
to the centre of the pane.
The light played around and almost through it,
a living pliqué-a-jour.

Smooth adherence of animal courage, tensioned
to the treacherous vertigo.
Frilled edges gripped, careful pitons, translucent
in the cool sunshine.

A paced adventure in abnormal gravity on
a bizarre, upended ice-rink.
Some freeze-framed slow tango of delight
from its silent accordion.

Now slowly turns, traversing to a new oblique
direction; for what reason?
Thinks better of it, begins a loop-the-loop,
then turns again.

Pauses, glued halfway below the glazing bar;
a far summit within its technique?
The coiled shell like a packed parachute,
for safety? or escape?

To the young child, viewing from the inside,
the quest was discerned
in simplest critique: "Look, Mummy,
that snail's flying!"

Th' Owd Mill

Ay, ah'm raight glad a'v <u>seed thi, Nell</u>!　　　　*seen you, Nell*
Shall yer cum, an' <u>we'en gu furra wark</u>?　　　*we'll go for a walk*
<u>Wut gu dairn</u> t'bruk 'n th'owd mill, Nell?　　*Will you go down*
Shall'st buth gu <u>'gether 'n tark</u>?　　　　　*together and talk*

An' wa <u>dus' tha tek mi fer nair</u>, lad?　　　*What do you take me for*
An' why iver dust wont wark <u>dairn theer</u>?　　*down there*
<u>Ar dunna wont</u> gu neer t'th'owd mill,　　　*I don't want*
Eet's '<u>aunted</u>, so's mill-pond, an th'<u>weer</u>.　　*It's haunted, weir*

Tha'rt spinnin' on owd wives' tales, Nell!
Eet's o' <u>sa mitch goster and sham</u>.　　　　*so much gossip and lies*
Just a wark along th'banksyde wi me, Nell,
<u>We'en non 'aff</u> gu neer th'owd dam.　　　　*We'll not have to*

Nay, <u>fer shuer a conna</u> du that, lad,　　　　*for sure I cannot*
A'm <u>frabbed</u>, an' munna gu neer.　　　　　*anxious*
An' we'en <u>non av sa mitch</u> fer tark abairt,　*not have so much*
'Cos am <u>fritten o</u>' wot went off theer.　　　*frightened of all*

Then <u>'appen we'en</u> tark abairt uz, Nell,　　*perhaps we'll*
That'll be th'easiest fert' du.
Then p'r'aps jus' sit 'n <u>'owd 'ands</u> a bit,　　*hold hands*
Jus' th'two on uz, <u>mey sut wi yuw</u>.　　　　*me sat with you*

Well, <u>o'raight</u> then, a s'pose <u>a mit</u>, lad,　　*alright, I might*
Nair <u>tha's exed</u> an' tha's <u>coddled</u> mi tu.　*you've asked,   coaxed*
<u>Bur'al oney</u> jus' cum ter th'bruksyde,　　　*but I'll only*
If that's <u>wit tha wonts</u> mi fert' du.　　　　*what you want*

121

Cum straightway nair wi me, Nell!
An' gi' mi thi <u>lesh</u> little 'and.   *smooth*
A'm glad tha's <u>finely</u> sed yes ter mi   *finally*
Tha meks mi raight <u>praired</u> an' grand.   *proud*

Nair <u>dunna</u> be gyettin' <u>sa frim</u>, lad,   *don't, so fresh*
Am non one o' them <u>frowsy</u> sorts.   *fancy*
Tha'd best bey a bit <u>muer</u> respec'ful,   *more*
Dus tha think a'l tek any owd <u>orts</u>?   *rubbish*

Dunna fling thi <u>glib slarts</u> at mey, Nell!   *easy insults*
Fer ah'm jus' as <u>jonnock</u> as thee.   *honourable*
Beside, tha's no naid be <u>fritten</u>, Nell,   *no need to be frightened*
A'l tek <u>cyaire</u> on thi fer rest o'th'dee.   *care*

Fair enuff, let's gu if tha wants, lad,
<u>Bur oney</u> as fer as th'bruk.   *but only*
Th'owd mill's <u>orlis</u> dark an'sa gloomy,   *always*
A reck'n eet's a place o' bad luck.

Wha' dust <u>thar naioo</u> abairt th'mill, Nell?   *you know*
An' ow <u>cos</u> tell o as went on?   *can you*
Nob'dys lived theer fer 'undred yeer,
The'en o <u>flit, ilse</u> o <u>jed</u> an' gone.   *all moved, else, dead*

Sum owd miller wunce lived at eet, lad,
an' 'is naym, thee <u>sen</u>, wur Mad John.   *said*
An' 'is wife gid birth ter a <u>chance-childt</u>,   *bastard*
<u>Burrit werna</u> nairt du wi' owd John.   *but it wasn't*

Sa tell me, whar'appened then, Nell?
Thar <u>ain't 'ayf</u> grippin' mi 'and!   *not half*
Tha lukes like thas cum <u>o'er gloppent</u>!   *become dumbstruck*
Th'art tremblin'an' <u>conna</u> seem stand!   *cannot*

Ay stop! We'er <u>neely</u> at'th'mill, lad! *nearly*
<u>O i'</u> darkness, wi' moonlight onth' <u>treys</u>! *all in, trees*
An' th' millstones ar grindin' an' grindin'!
Luke ow th'wayter's ripplin' in'th' <u>braize!</u> *breeze*

Thus nob'dy 'ere 'ceptin' uz, Nell,
An' th'sun's high-shinin' i'th'sky.
Th'mill-pond's o calm an' still a' glass,
Lay on't <u>gress</u> wi mi, dunna thi cry. *grass*

<u>Fower</u> tragedies o 'appened 'ere, lad! *four*
Mad John drownt that childt, then 'is wife!
'E shot dead th' <u>puer</u> lad as 'ad lay wi' 'er! *poor*
Then slit 'is own throat wi' a knife.

'Ow cum tha noes o' abairt this, Nell?
An' wot's eet <u>gyet du nair</u> wi thay? *got to do now*
A fear thuz summat abairt o this,
Thas non finished off tellin' mey.

Ay! Av towd thee o abairt eet, lad!
Coz a' tell thee ev'ry dey!
<u>Th' fower that's 'auntin'</u> this owd mill! *the four that's hunting*
Mad John, <u>mar</u> childt, mey an' they! *my*

P. Holland

Welcome to Britain

Welcome!
We'll share our miserable climate with you,
we'll share our foggy moors and barren hills,
we'll share our treacherous bogs and quicksands.
Will you help us cut wood for frozen times?
Come in!
You can share our hovels and stinking middens,
you can share our harsh days, sit huddled through the nights.
You can help hunt for food and fish our dangerous tides.
Will you be fearless, brave like us, and still survive?
Please stay!
Give us some order, purpose, and show us how to live,
give us your knowledge, and tell us how to build,
give us trade and commerce, bring us your prosperity.
Our Gods have left us, will yours be any better?
Be warned!
Here is lawlessness, our leaders fight amongst themselves.
Here, harvests are fickle and we quarrel with each other.
Here, we are suspicious of our neighbours, we hardly speak.
Will you show us how to live like decent men?
Wait!
You want everything that we have?
What? We are ungrateful and are no longer viable?
What? We cannot learn, and are not worth the effort?
What? We have no courage, manners, dignity?
No!
You only want us for your slaves!
We shun your roads and laws and taxes!
We don't need your baths and perfumes!
We don't want your wine or olives!
Bugger off, Romans!

Sue by Lucien *(version 1)*

Her flesh lolls,
bulked anima paused.
Thick paint spreads over the canvas,
like her ponderous weight supported on the upholstery.
A massed life, asleep. Her rich, full breasts find their new position;
belly and thighs relax to comfortable gravity; arms akin to a pregnant crab's limbs.
There is something of the fecundity of ripe pumpkin, or pungent slabs of lamb's liver.
Colours of the earth-mother: pink-browns, white clays, blue-greys in shadowed valleys;
tousled hair becomes an organic growth that haloes her mooned face and crescent neck.
She is beautiful; amoebic complexity of inanimation, a gloriously nascent-speckled rest.
Like some tired queen bee filled with royal jelly, she could suddenly burst into life;
some tight pomegranate bloat of seed, cocooned in the sofa's gentle effleurage.
Caressed by the artist's brush she is slowly flayed to his montage of creativity,
moulded to the eye's curious watch, and swayed in a banner of motionless awe.
Her voice comes through the headphones, pleasant, a manner of matter-of-factness.
I fear she may awake and reproach the viewers standing in her court; the loud tactless
comment; a sniggering voyeur; some shocked primness that brings ridiculous outrage.
But most are there to wonder and pay respect, see her image through miraculous insight.
The artist brings us to his feast and we may gorge. He shows us what we need to know,
her secrets are secure; the paint speaks that she is one of us. Sue's commentary stops.
Watching the intent faces looking, I have a sense of mutual bonding. We are like her:
father impregnated, mother nurtured, veins linking, muscles touching, skin shedding;
once fed through the very same omphalos of life, centred in continuation, sleep stilled.
Yet here is a quiet magnificence of art that takes a step back to look, really look, filled
with forensic wonder and a reverenced connection. Where is the first brushstroke?
Where the last? We know her so well now, but her dreams we cannot touch.
She is more magnificent than Sheba! Compare Venus, far too pale!
But Sue keeps on sleeping, oblivious to these comparisons.
The sofa waits, holding her in its palm.
Her flesh sleeps on.

The above lines were composed to form a 'picture poem' of Lucien Freud's painting; "Benefits Supervisor Sleeping" 1995. ('Big Sue' Tilley lies naked on a sofa, sleeping.) I arranged my lines to give an effect of extreme fore-shortening. Viewing the poem almost flat and sideways from the left-hand margin, the effect may be seen. Those who have seen the painting will no doubt recall the composition. Unfortunately the lines of this version cannot fit on A5 paper, hence the very small font formatting. Version 2 - a different setting - is overleaf.

Sue by Lucien *(version 2)*

Her flesh lolls, bulked anima paused.
Thick paint spreads over the canvas,
like her ponderous weight supported on the upholstery.
A massed life, asleep.
Colours of the earth-mother;
pink-browns, white clays, blue-greys in shadowed valleys.
Tousled hair becomes an organic growth
which haloes her mooned face and crescent neck.

She is beautiful, amoebic complexity of inanimation
in glorious nascent-speckled rest.
Her rich, full breasts find their new position,
belly and thighs relax to comfortable gravity,
arms akin to a pregnant crab's limbs.
There is something of the fecundity of ripe pumpkin,
or pungent slabs of lamb's liver.

Like some tired queen bee filled with royal jelly
she could suddenly burst into life,
some tight pomegranate bloat of seed
cocooned on the sofa's gentle effleurage.

Caressed by the artist's brush
she is slowly flayed to his montage of creativity,
moulded to the eye's curious watch,
and swayed in a banner of motionless awe.

Her voice comes through the headphones;
pleasant, a manner of matter-of-factness.
I fear she may awake in the picture
and reproach the viewers standing in her court;

the loud tactless comments, a sniggering voyeur,
some shocked primness that brings a ridiculous outrage.
But most are there to wonder and pay respect,
see her image through his profound insight.
The artist brings us to his feast so we may gorge.
He shows us what we need to know,
but her secrets are secure.
The paint speaks that she is one of us.

Sue's commentary stops.

Watching the intent faces looking,
I have a sense of mutual bonding, we are like her;
father impregnated, mother nurtured,
veins linking, muscles touching, skin shedding,
once fed through the very same omphalos of life,
centred in continuation, sleep stilled.

For here is a quiet magnificence of art
which takes a step back to look, really look,
filled with forensic wonder
and a reverenced connection.
Where the first brushstroke? Where the last?
We know her so well now,
but her dreams we cannot touch.

She is more magnificent than Sheba!
Compare Venus; far too pale!
But Sue keeps on sleeping,
oblivious to these comparisons.

The sofa waits, holding her in its palm.
Her flesh sleeps on.

To a Grandchild

Another print can somehow be nearer.
We see it through a closer observation.
The original is too soon, too close for comfort;
leaves no room for objectivity.
Seeing the blood fresher, more vital,
with no scars that speak, we can be more honest;
be more kindly critical, even detached at times.
Be more knowing with that second chance,
that connection which is not totally our responsibility.
The next generation, which gives such comfort,
makes it all worthwhile - and may prove our value?
Subsequent prints somehow tell us more.
But is there more to know? The page is hardly written on,
the few words still jumbled, the journey hardly begun.
Yet there is that certainty, that surety;
the same hills will still be climbed, but differently.

How would we change things? We can never change them.
How can we forewarn? There is no forewarning.
The trials come randomly; the tests come altered.
We can be sure of only one thing:
that the blood will sing its own song,
and come from a different heart.
This link of flesh, of mind, of genes, what of it?
Our form is transmutable, transferable,
copied merely as a human body, another printing.
The bonds are inexplicable, yes, even to science.
For the soul, the spirit, call it what you will, is a living thread;
a thread of family, of place, of teaching, of belonging.
Our comprehension falters at the why? the where? the when?
Can only the ties of blood and cells join us?

Each book is different; each life unique - but not separate.
Each of us is independent, yet linked forward and back.
That small matter of biology forges: the intake of breath,
the nurture, food, shelter, care, companionship, and love.
The stepping-stones coax the learning, problems, solutions;
all these, and the passing-on, the replication, the imprint.

But the most important imprint is love.
Science cannot explain love,
but Grandparents can.

Gull

And still you follow,

circling deck and rails,
cutting across wires and funnels;
a white, curved cross, high over waves,
then low in the troughs, empowered in your element.

Ultimate-wind-surfer,
webs hidden, wheeling with the currents,
close-shadowing us; guiding like a natural pilot,
an unelected escort to the larger westward scope.

Clear and cold your eye,
watching the wake. Wing-nudging the prow,
correcting, trimming, making sure of our leaving.
Telling us to go, or reminding us to return?

Lifting your out-riggers in ease,
turning your sternum to catch the drift,
cleaving your bill to the compass of unseen stars,
full-knowing all those maps salt-scored by ancient whales.

And what of the gaunt, receding mountains?
They can only watch, watch in a haughty suspicion.
Where, at their shoreline, they glower, blacker and harsher.
And farther back, an iron-grey bruising, less concerned,
and still farther back, higher, at the eye's ultimate fix,
merely an austere good-riddance, farewell of blue.

Wave-skimmer, crest-rider;
un-anchored, you measure the knots,
counting the fathomed fish below.

Why follow at all, why waste your time?
Do you really need for our company?
Are we your only friend?

Sheer and solitary, on you sail,
rowing the mists and spray.
Till, at last, after fjords and mountains
merge to the sea, and the last seal island fades
in the slipping sun,
suddenly, without a sign,
you are gone,

and we are alone.

Endgame

In these years,
after dystocia, bicycle scrapes,
puberty, love, loss and all the other illnesses,
we come, finally, to death.
The one we can't avoid.
No point in not talking about it;
it will, must, happen and sooner than we'd like;
though perhaps for one or two an option?

We play the rules and move our pieces on the board,
and hit the button on the timing clock,
then wait for God or Fate to hit it back.
Your move, I think.
We put on different clothes,
faces, each scene a newer, yet older, character,
adding up the milestones, the shorter days.
A walk-on part that wears off and then gets written out.

But still: that chance to be included
is surely what we treasure most.
Team-players who get sent off early still win,
and only lose that unappealingness of certainty.
To be a corpse; one who was so vital once,
one who ran, and laughed, and sat to talk,
even quarrelled and 'what's-the-point'ed...
is it just game over?

In these years, after two lots of nappies,
three lots of teeth, and several new joints;
learning - and forgetting - how to play,
finally the whistle blows. We rest. Life doesn't.

Needlewoman

This link is hers.
Her thread entwines,
though captures none.
In sharp end of life,
with a knowing eye,
she pierces memory.

Christening shawl,
Fair Isle socks,
wedding dress,
Winter mittens,
bed-ridden sheets;
she darns them all.

She pricks conscience,
yet allows the camel.
Wraps some cotton
around her ring
when that finger
has grown thin.

She joins the years
and mends the holes
of wear and tear.
And when her eyes
are in the shade
waits for her shroud.

Echoes

Oh! Swallow, swallow
bring sweet Spring!

"Swt-swt" swallow
all Summer sings.

Blow! Sallow bellows,
gold Autumn brings.

Go! Sweet swallow,
cold Winter stings.

Susurrus follows
far-flying wings.

"Swt-swt" echoes,
sweet echoing.

....and death?

It isn't just the doing, the stillness, lack of breath,
for I shall be oblivious in the moment after death.
My loved ones will be saddened, but for themselves, not me,
and those who are already gone, perhaps I'll join in harmony.
It isn't just the losing, for I shall surely nothing need,
my house to me now worthless and the books I used to read.
My friends may say they're sorry, those left may shed a tear,
but I can give no comfort, or even tell them not to fear.

It isn't just the coming, the dread, the letting go,
for I shall have no work to do, nor have a need to know.
My enemies might grin and gloat, and call me fool, or knave,
but I'll know something that they don't, having passed the grave.
I know that I'll be sad to go, leave children, darling wife,
but it's simply that I've stopped rowing the waters of my life.
My pen, so soon a rusty thing, whose ink so often over-flowed,
yet I hope to be remembered for some kindnesses I showed.

It isn't that I'm frightened, though death will surely try,
I'll break his scythe and hour-glass then laugh until I cry!
My life has been so wonderful, like some never-fading flower,
yet seasons still will surely come, though this my final hour.
It isn't that I want to go, though one day I must, not may,
till then, I'll put it off a bit, too much to do today!
I've tried to give throughout my life, be true to all I know,
so I'll not mind when death appears, and says "It's time to go."

It's not about the dying part that my last thought will be,
but knowing that I lived and loved the people dear to me!
Till then I'll struggle on and with my last lungful of breath,
I hope to grin and try to bellow, "Get behind me, death!"

Jigsaw (*reprise*)

My jigsaw now looks back at me complacently;

an irony, as there are still those unmade pieces.

Perhaps I will not look too quickly for them;

take my time, live these last few years more carefully,

hope the trickling sand may block and stop.

Shall I make the last few shapes with a reverence?

Paint them in those colours that are slow to dry?

Take the gnomon from the dial and stall for time?

Well, one day the last piece must be fitted,

if not by me, then hopefully by someone.

This jigsaw is unique to me, with all its blemishes;

the picture on the box is as it happened.

To cut it into shapes and mix them seems a travesty,

the trawling and scanning compounds the pity.

Pack the pieces back in the box for someone else to fit!

Perhaps the puzzle may be solved by those with time to spare?

- *Notes & Glossary* -

Pg:

20 Jigsaw - some insights and reflections.

DNA; Deoxyribonucleic acid. A self-replicating material as a nucleic acid containing the genetic instructions used in the development and functioning of all known living organisms. The DNA segments, especially as constituent chromosomes, carry this information and are called genes. As discovered by Francis Crick and James D. Watson, DNA is arranged in a double helix cell formation.

Turkish rug; generally speaking the hand-made rugs of the ancient Turkish, Persian and Central Asian areas utilized two types of knots. The western areas, especially around Anatolia, used the symmetrical '*ghiordes*' double knot, known as the 'Turkish knot'. Each knot is made on two warps resulting in a stronger rug than the more typical asymmetrical '*senneh*' single knot which is referred to as the 'Persian knot' which is typical to Central Asia. The oldest known hand-knotted rug was found in the Pazyryk burials of the Scythian people in Siberia dating to the 5th century B.C.

22 Baltic Dawn - for Julie and Stephen Collins, when cruising with them on the "MSC *Jewel of the Seas*" towards St. Petersburg.

23 Solmonath - for Michael Le-Baigue, a friend and fellow dialect-enthusiast.

chommered, (chommered-up) : A Derbyshire White Peak dialect word to describe the churned-up state of sodden fields or water-logged farm-tracks.

hask : another local dialect word to describe a cold, bitter, dry, 'searching' wind. The phrase would be; "Eet wur 'n 'ask wind as'd cut thi i'taioo!" This roughly translates into; "It was a bitter wind that would cut you in two!" The 'ai' (as in air) and 'oo' (as in you) is pronounced as a diphthong.

Solmonath; the Pre-Christian Anglo-Saxon word for the month equivalent to the Roman (and modern) February is *Solmonath; Sol* meaning mud, or earth, and *monath* meaning month. So it may be literally translated as '*Mudmonth*'. In Bede's 'On *the Reckoning of Time*', written 725 A.D., he writes in chapter 15: '*Solmonath can be called "month of cakes", which they offered to their gods in that month*'. This alludes to the pagan practise of burying cakes in the earth to 'purify' it at the time of Spring ploughing. This *Aecerbot*, or Field Remedy, was an Old English charm to make a field fertile. The practise is recorded in early 10th and 11th century manuscripts, and Bede's earlier mention arguably goes back to this English custom.

24 Weasel - remembering Jack Perkins, a gamekeeper on the Warslow moors.

alizarin : a red colouring that is obtained from the Madder plant which may be used in paint pigment or as a dye in the textile industry. *Alizarine* (French) from *alizari* coming from the Arabic '*isãra*' (pressed juice) and from '*asara*' (to press fruit).

madder : (*Rubia Tinctorum)* – a herbaceous plant with yellowish flowers. A red dye may be taken from its crushed roots. Etymologically, the word comes from the Old English – *mædere*.

25 Swallow - written at Chinley Independent Chapel, High Peak.

Red Arrows; the famous, daring and incomparable Royal Air Force flying formation team.

Mercator, Gerardus; Flemish cartographer who presented his world map projection in 1569. This was used for many years for nautical purposes and relies on its usage in '*constant course*' by using *rhumb* lines, or *loxodromes*, in straight segments.

26 Metamorphosis - at Clay Cross, a coal-mining village in Derbyshire.

Sikorsky : designers, builders and exporters of some of the world's most advanced helicopters, used for commercial, industrial and military purposes. The company is still based in Stratford, Connecticut, U.S.A.

Spielbergian : of, or pertaining to, the style, character and brilliance of Stephen Spielberg, the celebrated American film director and producer.

Kafka, Franz : lived from 1883 to 1924. Kafka was born to a middle-class Ashkenazy Jewish family in Prague. His works are recognised as seminal in the canon of International literature. He wrote many novellas, the principally known one being '*Die Verwandlung*' (*The Metamorphosis*) The main protagonist is Gregor Sansa, a travelling salesman, who wakes to find himself transformed into a hideous giant insect.

27 Miss Morrissey - eavesdropping on a trio.

29 Snail and Shell - after re-reading D.H. Lawrence's poetry; especially the *'Birds, Beasts and Flowers'* in "*The Complete Poems*" (Heinemann, 1964)

30 Rope - for Edward, my son, a Tug-O-War athlete.

31 Rubáiyát - Oliver Gomersal's gift to me of a early 19th century illustrated copy of "*The Rubáiyát of Omar Khayyám*".

Rubáiyát (singular: Rubái) : short four-line verses of intense poetry as immortalized in the above book. The Persian poet known as Omar Khayyám, lived 1048 – 1123, was also a mathematician and astronomer, and reputedly wrote over 1,000 *Rubáiyát*. These were famously translated by Edward Fitzgerald, amongst others, and popularised in Victorian times. Not all literary critics agree to the merit or validity of these translations, but Fitzgerald's were, arguably, the best. A *'rubai '* poem has a rhyming scheme *a, a, b, a.* , The shortness of the poem is delineated and enhanced by the intensity of the language chosen within it.

Fool's gold; iron pyrites. Historically, often mistaken by over-excited prospectors and pan-handlers for real gold because of its sparkling colour

32 Curlew - on "*The Knabbs*", a marshy field at Glutton Grange.

Job; ancient seer mentioned in the Bible and the Qur'an. As a Hebrew prophet Job is resigned to being sorely tested by God by gradually having everything taken away from him and then being allowed to be tempted by the Devil. Job endures all these losses and afflictions without ever once losing his faith. Unfortunately, in much later interpretations, Job is incorrectly presented as a pathetically morose and pessimistic loner, rather than the steadfast man.

34 Watch - at "*J. Sidebotham & Son*", Buxton. A true happening.

35 Tell me a story - for Elizabeth, my daughter.

Ali Baba; some critics claim that the story of '*Ali Baba and the Forty Thieves'* was spuriously added to that convoluted collection of medieval Arabic literature; '*One Thousand and One Nights'*, by one of the latter's translators, Antoine Gallard, an 18th century French writer. The theme of Ali Baba is of the honest man who benefits from finding stolen treasure hidden in a cave guarded by the magical stone, '*Sesame'*. The story is linked to pantomime themes, especially "*Aladdin*", and was used as a base for the musical, "*Chu Chin Chow*" in 1916.

37 Equus - on seeing Peter Schaeffer's play.

Written in 1973, this disturbing drama tells the story of a psychiatrist attempting to treat a dysfunctional seventeen year old youth who has cruelly blinded horses in his care. The pathological, sexual, religious and Oedipal themes to do with the youth are juxtaposed against the psychiatrist's professional, personal and marital problems.

centaur; a mythological creature; half man, half horse.

38 Funny - bitter-sweet lyrics for a song.

39 Boy on a stone trough - an old photograph above my bed.

40 Yew - "*.....that yew tree's shade,"* - a half-line from Thomas Gray's *'Elegy Written in a Country Churchyard.'* written in 1750 and published 1751

Albion, coming from the Greek language, is the oldest known and most archaic name for Great Britain. Poetically, it more specifically refers to England. The name has been used by many classical writers; Pliny the Elder, in his "*Natural History*", wrote: "*It was itself named Albion, while all the islands about which we shall soon briefly speak are called Britanniae.*"

Ptolemy, writing in the 2nd century A.D., uses the name '*Albion'* in his *"Geographia"* instead of the Roman word *'Brittania'*, possibly following the commentaries of Marinus of Tyre.

As a boy I remember my father and grandfather talking about a rare breed of cattle called 'Blue Albions'. They had blue-ish grey mottlings on a white background, sometimes with solid-coloured spots, similar to a blue-merle spaniel's colouring. They also had short, inward-curving horns. Some claimed they were an ancient, definite and separate breed, others said they were probably a cross between roan Shorthorns and the earliest Friesian cattle originally imported from the Low Countries. I certainly recall seeing odd specimens occasionally in the cattle markets, and sometimes four or five in a herd of fifty in the more traditional home-bred enclosed herds.

41 Slow Burn - at "*Gardner's*" scrap yard in Dove Holes, near Buxton.

Iron Maiden; a traction engine constructed by the engineer J. Fowler which was built in 1920. It was later re-named and featured in a British comedy film of the same name in 1962

Model T; from September 1908 to October 1927 Henry Ford's Motor Company produced the famous 'Model T' motor car. Affectionately known as the 'Tin Lizzie', the car offered affordable automotive travel to middle-class America, and eventually the rest of the world.

Ark Royal; there have been five warships named *Ark Royal* in the British Navy. The first was the flagship of the English Fleet at the time of the Spanish Armada in 1588. The last was *H.M.S. Ark Royal (R07)*, an aircraft carrier launched in 1981 and finally decommissioned in 2011.

Concorde; this Anglo-French supersonic passenger airliner first flew in 1969. With its iconic delta wing and adjustable nose cone, Concorde was capable of carrying 120 passengers at Mach 2.04 (1,350 m.p.h.) The environmental issues, coupled with its one and only disastrous, though blameless, crash, made it financially unviable and it was finally retired in 2003.

AK47; this very efficient selective-fire, gas-operated assault rifle was first developed by Mikhail Kalashnikov in the U.S.S.R. soon after the end of 1945. It was, and still is, a highly-prized standard military issue weapon all over the world.

42 Foxfire - from a farming memory on Park House Hill, Glutton Grange.

44 Aubade - after reading the poems in the "*Larkin's England*" Concert at the Buxton Festival, 2010, together with Ian Buckle, the concert pianist, who had arranged the programme of Larkin's poetry and contemporary piano music.

aubade; strictly describes a love song in the morning from a door or window to a sleeping woman, (as opposed to a *serenade* which appertains to the evening). An *aubade* is more generally known as a composition, both musically as well as linguistically, which generally evokes daybreak.

47 Coming into Amsterdam - whilst cruising on "MSC Opera", 4.00 a.m.

Hitchcock, Alfred, 1899 -1980; one of the most famous British film directors, Hitchcock is synonymous with the genre of psychological thriller and horror movies. He made 50 films, amongst which are the likes of *'The Lady Vanishes'*, *'North by Northwest'*, *'Notorious'*, *'The Birds'* and, arguably his masterpiece, *'Psycho'*. The term *'Hitchcockian'* is recognised as an accolade for any emulating film of this genre.

Falstaff; the rotund, verbose, gluttonous, drunken, yet lovable rogue who appears in no less than three of Shakespeare's plays.

guilder; a coin, an ancient, though now obsolete, monetary unit of the Netherlands

Schengen; the original Schengen Agreement, a *'borderless travel and trade group'* within the European Union, was signed in 1995. The first signatories were: Belgium, France, Luxembourg, The Netherlands and West Germany. Arguably, it was considered by some as a protectionist elite within the larger organisation. Some are more equal than others.

50 A breath of fresh air - on a house clearance.

antimacassar; usually made of linen and often embroidered, these pieces of textile, about half the size of a tea towel, were often draped over the headrests of chairs and sofas. A fussy Victorian mode of protecting the main upholstery fabric from being soiled by macassar oil, which was commonly used by fashionable gentlemen as a hair tonic.

majolica; originally a white, tin-glazed earthenware decorated with metallic colours which was popular in the Mediterranean during the Renaissance. There was a revival of the ware during the Victorian period, and it is still made today. Coming from the Italian former name of Majorca.

51 Helmikuu - a Finnish word for the month of February. It translates as *'Month of the Pearl'* and refers to the *'February Rattle';* the icy wind blowing through branches hung with icicles. From the end of January through February and early March, the extreme Finnish Winter weather may occasionally thaw for a very brief period before freezing hard again. The temporary drops of moisture on the twigs of trees melt and freeze alternately giving the impression of pearls which 'rattle' in the wind.

52 Kite - on a visit to Wales.

Darwin, Charles Robert; lived from 1809 to 1882. Famous English anthropologist, scientist and free thinker. During a five year world-wide voyage in *H.M.S. Beagle*, Darwin finally crystallized his research and ideas during a stay on The Galapagos Islands. He then published his radical "*On the Origin of Species by Means of Natural Selection*", in 1859. Though a shocked public and an antagonistic Church reviled his theories, the term '*Darwinism*' is still universally recognised as one of the most important studies of evolution.

Red Baron, The; his actual name was Manfred Albrecht Freiherr von Richthofen. Famous German First World War fighter pilot. Awarded the 'Blue Max', the highest Prussian medal. Forever synonymous with his red- painted Fokker Dr. 1 triplane, von Richthofen was a propaganda hero who, whilst credited with very high 'kill' rates, arguably didn't reach the total of 80 or so aeroplanes *'shot down'*, which was often claimed.

Icarus; son of Daedalus in Greek mythology. As they were both escaping from King Minos of Crete using wings made from feathers held together by wax, Icarus was warned by his father not to fly too near the sun. Tragically, Icarus was the victim of his own hubris; ignoring his father's advice, the wax melted, he fell and was drowned in the sea.

Wallis, Barnes; aeroplane designer and also inventor of the famous '*Bouncing Bomb*' in W.W.11 which was employed in the successful Bomber Command '*Dambusters*' operation, thus paralyzing the Nazi industrial region of the Ruhr valley.

Linnaeus, Carl; the Swedish botanist, physician and zoologist regarded as the father of taxonomy. He lived between 1707 and 1778 and was largely responsible for the classification of plants and animals in what is now known as binomial nomenclature

55 Poppies - a series of haiku. Classically, the Japanese haiku form of poetry is of three intense lines of 5, 7 and 5 syllables respectively.

56 Utstein Kloster - a visit to the island of Mosterøy.

Norway's best preserved medieval monastery is set on an island in Rogaland. Augustinian monks were established there by 1160. Now an important tourist attraction, it may be reached by an underground tunnel.

63 On a cousin ill - last meeting with Don Holland, a cousin.

"...the ripest fruit first falls, and so doth he." - Richard 11, Act 11. Sc 1.

strike; a local word meaning an archaic weighed measurement of boxed fruit; especially plums and damsons. Officially it is two bushels, though some argue 80lbs in weight; others say 40lbs. A '*strickle*' or '*strickler*' being the metal tool which is used to level off the heaped box of fruits, berries or even grain, etc. A phrase using the word may be phonetically illustrated in Derbyshire dialect as : " *'E gid mi a strike a damson.*" – 'He gave me a strike of damsons.' The "*a damson*", rather than "*o' damson*", and the *singular*, rather than the *plural* fruit, being the more typical local idiom of speech.

Victoria; - a breed of English plum. A cultivar from the egg plum group, *Prunus domestica*. Named after Queen Victoria, 1819 -1901, the species was first discovered in a garden in Alderton, Sussex.

64 Arboretum - for Roger Elkin, written when attending one of his poetry courses at Wedgwood College, Barlaston.

wodwo; literally a "*wildman of the woods*". A mythological being attributed to the forest, similar to a faun or satyr. Connected to the magical fables of "*The Green Man*", a theme which is contained in early mediaeval art and literature. Also the title of a book of poetry by Ted Hughes.

66 - Sounds - for Ian Buckle, the concert pianist, thinking about his playing in his "*Larkin's England*" and "*Housman - Shropshire and other lads*" Concerts in the Buxton and Chester Festivals, 2010, 2011 and 2012.

67 Skins - various images.

Dhobi; the name for a washerman or washerwoman in the Indian sub-continent. An unfortunate affliction of the skin often affects such people and is known as '*the dhobi itch*'. A similar scabrous mange may affect people, and cattle, in Europe. It is highly contagious and is referred to as '*ringworm*', though no worms are present. The affliction manifests itself in circular lesions.

Pinchbeck, Christopher; an 18th century English clockmaker, who invented a brass-like alloy made from copper and zinc which resembled gold. He used it to make cheap costume jewellery which was stamped with his name. Inevitably, it soon began to be passed off as real gold by spurious tradesmen.

68 Flagg Races - with the Mackenzie family.

Flagg is a village in the White Peak of Derbyshire. Here, a famous Point to Point race meeting is run traditionally on Easter Tuesday organised by the High Peak Hunt. The horses are raced on a temporary course over stone walls and brush fences on exposed farmland. Historically, there have been many times when snow and fog have caused great problems, although the diehards have continued to brave the elements since 1892. The spectators stand on a prominent limestone escarpment with superb views of the entire course and spectacular countryside.

Pegasus; 'The Winged Horse'. Supposedly born of a union between Poseidon and Medusa, there are various stories about this fantastical beast in

Greek mythology. In one, Pegasus was ridden by Bellerophon when he slew the Chimera and also the Amazons.

69 Pavane for Vera - Commissioned by Linda Harry, i.m. of her mother.

pavane; a slow, measured dance, usually of calm, resigned or even slightly sad disposition. Known for its stateliness, the figure is danced in slow duple time, in pairs, and was originally a slow, processional dance form popular in 16th century Europe. Performed in the elegant, voluminous clothing of the time, the participants would walk forward, slightly lift their leg and point the toe. Popular with courtly people to show off their elaborate clothes. The origin of the word may be from the Italian *"Padovana"* - a dance typical of the Paduan region, or even possibly from the Spanish *"pavón"* - peacock. The music composed for it is also known as a Pavane. Probably the most well-known piece of music associated with this dance is Maurice Ravel's *"Pavane pour une infante défunte"* composed in 1899.

69 Leafing through pages - for Andrew Mackenzie-Wicks, the tenor.

71 Giraffe - a silly one for all my grandchildren.

camelopard; from '*Camelopardalis*', the Latin Romanization of the name for the giraffe, originally coming from the Greek language - i.e. a camel, but with spots like a leopard.

72 First cockerel - around the hen cotes at Glutton Grange.

73 Twelve - for Rev. John Hudghton, Rural Dean in Buxton.

Simon Peter - 'Cephas' is the Aramaic word for rock, 'Petra' being the Greek word for it. 'Building sites' is suggesting Rome, i.e. the foundation of the Christian Church. 'Ear for music' is linked to what Peter cut off the Roman soldier in Gethsemane. Rock music; again the 'rock' motif . 'Pete and the Cockerels' suggests the three denials Peter uttered after the arrest of Jesus, after which a cock crowed. These are the 'three big hits' he scored.

Andrew – 'Scottish' connection; a coastal crofter seemed to fit the 'Fishers of Men' link. Is he possibly gay, or just a loner? The original Andrew was firstly the disciple of John the Baptist; my suggested 'friend' who goes to stay with Andrew. John the Baptist was later beheaded in 'a terrible accident', which alludes to Salome. Andrew becomes a recluse after losing his friend and mentor.

James – He is known as 'one of the sons of thunder' John, his brother, no.4, being the other one. They were both very headstrong, *Boanerges* was the family name: hence 'all B.O. and energy'. A blacksmith seemed to fit him somehow, even as the drunkard and wife-beater. But he has a good side; sexton of the Churchyard, and still missing his Dad.

John - A policeman, a racist, and a male stripper out for some hard cash, but loathing the raucous 'Essex' girls who pay for his performance, and secretly wondering at, and admiring, the absence of Muslim women. The recent London riots seemed a good place to anchor him. Although he does care and worry about his children.

Philip – A petty thief, trying to justify his actions. His name in Greek means a lover of horses; the gambling race-goer seemed apt. He also likes his women, a lot, but he has a good side, 'giving' his mum the stolen goods, 'passed it over' is suggesting The Passover.

Bartholomew – Negro Spiritualist who steals from the collection plate. He hopes God will forgive him, but keeps on doing it. 'Skin' is an issue with him, 'give the black man some skin' - skin being slang for dollars, also the 'High Five!' greeting. The original Bartholomew was skinned alive as depicted in the famous painting by Michelangelo in the Sistine Chapel, which depicts St. Bartholomew holding his own skin.

Matthew - The tax gatherer, he works for the Romans - 'render unto Caesar that which is Caesar's'. I also jibe at the modern 'off shore' cowards. He is also a publican. Matthew is pious about alcohol, but still sells it for profit. He was a Levite, or Levi, a reactionary Jew of the day – hence he always wears Levi jeans in this modern portrayal.

Thomas – The Doubter. I make him a ventriloquist/clown, perhaps a Ken Dodd 'look-alike' - the 'Diddymen' chimed with Didymus, which is Aramaic for 'twin'. He was a twin in real life, so we are told. I thought the odd relationship between ventriloquist and dummy seemed apt. When Thomas says he will only believe Christ has risen if he can put his hand in his side was a bizarre image I couldn't get out of my head. Thomas is a self-doubter needing tangible proofs. Curiously, many clowns are often sad and insular, craving adulation and love.

James – Known as James the Less. We are told he went to Compostela and founded Christianity there, but it's all a bit vague. I thought the shy man at work seemed to typify him, everyone knows of him, but doesn't really know him. He was the son of Alphaeus, so the shorter common name Alf was included. James was also known as James the Just, so.... just James.

Thaddeus - also called Lebbaeus and Jude – another lesser disciple. In the Bible he is recorded as speaking only once, at the Last Supper – the 'going away party'. He is the Patron saint of all lost causes and hopeless cases. Hardy's "*Jude the Obscure*" is a portrayal of a ditherer, a no-hoper, a victim of his own prevarications. Not much else to say about you, hey Jude?

Simon - The Zealot; communist, radical, activist, freedom fighter. Always a thorn in the Romans' side. A big fish in a little pool – Hackney. His girlfriend is a 'blue-blood', he can't stand them really, but can she help his cause? She could be a kind of Mitford sister trophy to him? He needs a Vanessa Redgrave-type icon to champion him and his cause.

Judas – He works for the Local Authority, the 'Annas and Caiaphas Council' Judas was supposed to have been a charity worker. He objected to Mary Magdalene pouring the precious ointment, spikenard, onto the feet of Jesus. It could have been sold and given to the poor, so 'Chavs' and the 'because-you're-worth-it' syndrome seemed apt. The 'sensitive information' is the betrayal of Jesus, plus trousering the thirty silver pieces, all leading to his remorse and suicide by hanging himself from a thorn tree.

Jesus was said to have chosen his Disciples from simple men, all probably flawed in some way; after all they were human beings. But he chose them specifically; they all had the potential to change the world, and they did. It wasn't Jesus who spread Christianity, but his Disciples as Ambassadors; he spoke through them. All the Disciples were martyred in one way or another, except Judas. Even he, as a suicide, was a kind of martyr?

77 Love practically - for Pat, my wife.

77 Skylark - a sonnet for Sir Christopher Ball.

78 Masca - on holiday in Tenerife with Linda and John Harry. *Masca*; a small, remote village perched high in the Mascan Gorge of the Teno mountains on the island of Tenerife. Although it was a settlement for hundreds of years, the first road to it was only built in the 1960s. Previously, access took three hours via a tortuous walking track from a sea inlet far below.

Laocoön; a Trojan priest who angered the Gods by making love to his wife in a temple. When the attacking Greeks sent their Trojan Horse as a gift to Troy, Laocoön desperately argued that it was a trick, hence the old adage; *"Beware Greeks bearing gifts!"*. As a punishment for his misdemeanours the Gods sent two sea serpents which strangled Laocoön and also his twin sons, Antiphantes and Thymbraeus. There is a famous antique sculpture in the Vatican depicting this heroic but deadly struggle.

80 Two Fires - after re-reading some poetry of John Donne.

81 Fukushima - site of the ill-fated Japanese nuclear power station destroyed in the devastating earthquakes and subsequent tsunami on 11th March, 2011.

82 Our Jack - a satirical sketch on an annoying bird.

Hitler, Adolf; Austrian-born political fanatic who became the autocratic leader (*Der Führer*) of the German Nazis before and during

W.W.11. Originally an extreme Socialist who wrote his vile book, "*Mein Kampf*" (*'My Struggle'*) whilst in jail. He was the main architect and bears most responsibility for the Jewish Holocaust. Arguably, the most hated man in the history of the world. He committed suicide, with his lover, Eva Braun, in 1945. His father, allegedly Alois Schicklgruber, changed his surname to Hitler, which for his illegitimate son, Adolf, was probably a wise move, in so far as it is doubtful people could have possibly kept a straight face when expected to chant: "*Heil Schicklgruber*". He had a dreadful haircut and a worse moustache.

83 Bridge - on a suicide.

84 Fired clay - for Roger Elkin, after attending another of his excellent literary courses at Wedgwood College, Barlaston, where he was the tutor.

85 First breath - one of many I helped into the world.

hummering; Derbyshire dialect for the enclosed bleating in the throat that ewes give only when birthing their lambs, and at no other time.

86 May on Dove Banks - a seasonal sonnet.

Dove Banks; the steepish, south-facing pastures and woods in Earl Sterndale parish lying between Crowdecote and Pilsbury which front the River Dove on the Derbyshire/Staffordshire border.

87 The 'Glevum Economy' - thinking of my father, Frank Edward Holland, and my grandfather, Albert William Holland.

Glevum Economy; a patented egg incubator which was extant in the late Victorian and Edwardian times.

effleurage; from the French word *effleurer* – to skim. A light, gentle stroking massage with the palm of the hand, an old-fashioned soothing aid often used during childbirth.

demmick; arguably, a dialect word meaning a misfit, something not quite right, or a *'bad-doer'*. In poultry especially, those chicks which couldn't hatch out, or were malformed. When hens became old and scraggy they were also said to be 'demmicks'. A word used by Mancunian Jewish poultry dealers, who, when buying old hens, would claim there were "*too many demmicks!*"

90 Wolf - on seeing the *'animalier'* paintings by Paul Tavenor.

91 Villanelle for Salvador Dali - after seeing the Dali Exhibition in County Hall, London, and thinking of his famous "*Persistence of Memory*" painting.

92 The Buxton Y.F.C. (Young Farmers Club**)** - thinking of the "*Plays and Entertainments*" I was involved in over many years.

D.E.F.R.A.; acronym for the Department for Environment, Food and Rural Affairs, replacing the older M.A.F.F. (Ministry of Agriculture, Fisheries and Food.) Yet another example of the totally unnecessary and expensive

Governmental '*re-branding*' of something that worked equally as inefficiently both before and afterwards. The official pebble in the farmer's boot!

93 North Sea - cruising on the "*Jewel of the Seas.*"

95 Peaklanders - commissioned by Alastair, Bishop of Derby for the occasion of the visit of the Archbishop of Canterbury, Dr. Rowan Williams, to The Farming Life Centre at Taddington, Derbyshire, 24/09/2011.

Peaklanders; historically, the Pennines were part of the Brigantes tribal lands. One of their famous queens was Cartimandua, who was, in the main, loyal to her Roman overlords. It was she who handed the resistance fighter, Caractacus, over to them in chains in 51 A.D., whence he was later humiliatingly paraded in Rome. Her first husband was Venutius, whom she divorced, then married his armour-bearer, Vellocatus, elevating him to king. In the 2nd century A.D. the Brigantes were written of in Ptolemy's '*Geographia*', and by the Roman poet, Juvenal, who writes of a father urging his son to '*gain glory by burning the forts of the Brigantes*'. Whilst there is no written record of the area before the Roman occupation, there is crucial evidence of a large Brigantian hill fort being burnt at Castle Hill, near Huddersfield, circa 430 B.C. Yet the perpetrators are unknown, as the event was well before the Roman Invasion of 43 A.D.

The Pecsætan – (Peaklanders, or *Peakrills*) were a later Anglo-Saxon tribe that inhabited the High Peak. These Pecsætan, originally spelt Pecsætna, were responsible for some early Derbyshire settlements. They were West Angles who forged up the Derwent and Dove valleys around the 7th century A.D. , these lands forming the northern edge of the even more ancient Mercian kingdom. The first Bishop of Mercia was Diuma, c.656, who brought Christianity to Derbyshire; Repton Abbey being built in 660.)

Lambeth; meaning Lambeth Palace, being the residence of the Archbishop of Canterbury. Used here as a personification of its incumbent.

96 Youth by Age - recognising both, finally.

97 Come March - remembering my father's birthday, the 1st of March.

frim; a High Peak dialect term describing the especially rich, lush greenness of Spring grass. There is a south-facing hillside at Earl Sterndale known as "*Frim Bank*".   My Grandfather used to say "*March dust is worth a guinea an ounce!*" meaning that the land was drying out by Spring winds and the time to work in the fields was possible. A saying proving its antiquity in using obsolete, archaic monetary and weight measure.

Similarly, in Dr. Samuel Pegge's celebrated *"Two Collections of Derbicisms"*, written in the second half of the 18th century, on pg.267 there is a note mentioning the saying; *'a peck of March Dust is worth a King's Ransom'*

snow-bones; in the Peak District Wintertime, after a prolonged covering of snow and then a thaw, these are the last remnants of drifts usually remaining under the north side of walls and hedges. With weak Winter sunlight too low in the sky there is not enough prolonged warmth to melt these stubborn relics. The local saying is that there will eventually have to be a bit more snow to come and take away these symbols of harsh days. March winds are usually the 'undertakers' after the last snow has fallen.

*wick***;** a Derbyshire High Peak dialect word meaning vigorous, sharp-spirited and able to thrive. Especially said in description of lambs which, after being born, quickly get to their feet, suckle and thrive in spite of harsh weather.

98 The Colonel - for the 'London Chums', remembering some wonderful times and memorable dinner parties together!

malts; special, highly-prized single distillations of whisky made from malted barley. Most ordinary brands of commercial blended whisky are made up of combinations of various and lesser qualities of malt or already blended whiskies. N.B. - the brands of malt whisky mentioned in the poem are all worthy of sampling. No preference or bias is suggested or implied. However, all omissions are regretted and unintentional.

N.B. - Port and tea are also mentioned in the poem, though merely once!

100 Elephant - from a childhood dream, rekindled at a zoo many years later.

purdah; that which is shielded from view; (also *'in purdah'* - in a state of protection or inaccessibility*)*. From the Persian language meaning *'curtain'*, and also *'honour'*.

musth; again coming from the Persian and meaning 'intoxication'; Also *'in musth'* , the seasonal testosterone-filled state of bull elephants, when a tar- like secretion called *temporin* discharges from the temporal glands. The bull elephant is particularly dangerous and highly unpredictable during such hormonal cycles.

102 Be still - for Graham Hinds, Agricultural Chaplain, at Bakewell Market.

104 Stoop - a challenge from Michael Le Baigue; a quick study in stone.

stoop: specifically, another name for an ancient stone guide post, milestone or waymarker. Derbyshire is particularly rich in these mainly sandstone or gritstone pillars set up as directional signposts. Owing to the slim, squarish nature of stoops, many towns have their spellings carved into the stone charmingly spanning more than one line! Also, more generally, any stone stump used for gate-hanging purposes.

106 Sweet Fruit - for a Feminist friend.

107 Sounds and senses - more stepping stones and recollections.

108 Ploughing the end of the line - for Sir Christopher Ball. After a spirited Sunday morning discussion on silly line endings in poetry, the pure affectation of such constructions, and the juxtaposition of the title of this poem to the failure in some University students' achievements!

110 Sire - for Edward, my son, remembering the bull-pens at Glutton Grange.
  beldering - local dialect for the bellow of a bull.

113 In a garden - preference, but no guarantee.
  Alzheimer's disease; a serious disorder of the brain which manifests itself in premature senility. Named after Alois Alzheimer, the German psychiatrist and neuropathologist, who first discovered it in 1906.

114 Christmas Rules, O.K.? Commissioned by Cllr. Robert Plant & Mrs. J. Plant, Mayor & Mayoress of Leek, Staffordshire.

115 To: janus@godsrus.com - for the Derbyshire "Stanza".

117 Requiem - listening to Duruflé and my boyhood conscience.
  Duruflé, Maurice; 1902 - 1986, celebrated French composer and organist. He entered the Paris Conservatoire in 1920. He was commissioned by Durand, the French music publishers, to write his '*Requiem*'. This became the most famous of his relatively small works, nevertheless his compositions, especially for organ, are regarded highly in the repertoire. He married Marie-Madeleine Chevalier, also a talented musician, in 1953 and they became a popular and famous organ duo. His most celebrated pieces are his '*Requiem*', 1947, and '*Mass*', 1967. Duruflé was very badly injured in a car accident in 1975, resulting in him having to retire from performing.

120 Plique-à-jour - for my grandson, Lewis Kinder Mackenzie.
  'Plique-à-jour' comes from the French language; literally *'glimpse of day'*. Also appertaining to *'letting in light'*, coming from the effect of the technique of setting translucent vitreous enamelling fired in backless cells bounded by gold or silver. It has a similar appearance to a stained glass effect, though much more difficult to achieve due to the lengthy processes and its extreme fragility. Originally a Byzantine craft from around 6th century A.D. which was unfortunately lost after the Mongol invasions of 13th Century. Russian aristocracy prized it in religious artefacts, objets d'art and decorative tableware. It usually exists only in small examples; icons, antiques, and some jewellery. Large pieces are extremely rare. The French term for such examples

appeared in the 14th C. (The later *'cloisonné'* process uses cells which are solid backed.) A Japanese form - *'shotai-shippo'* - dates from the 19th century. There is a similar modern process used in jewellery, but it is inferior in quality to the original processes.

121 Th' Owd Mill - a ballad told in the dialect around Glutton Bridge and set about 150 years ago. It isn't a true story, but it could be?

124 Welcome to Britain - thinking about those who couldn't write then.

125 Sue, by Lucien (*version 1*) - after seeing Lucien Freud's paintings in The National Portrait Gallery, 2012.

126 Sue, by Lucien, *(version 2)*

128 To a grandchild - commissioned by Jane Priestman, of Stretton Grandison, Herefordshire, for her grandson.

129 Gull - on leaving Norway.

131 Endgame - for Sir Christopher Ball.

   dystocia; difficult conditions or presentations at birth giving rise to prolonged parturition, thus increasing the chances of brain damage, due to oxygen starvation, or at worst, death.

132 - Needlewoman - remembering Alethea Naden, of Dove Cottage, Glutton Bridge, who used to knit jumpers and socks for me when I was little. Her mother, Mrs. Wheeldon also lived there. They had a huge case of stuffed birds and eggs in the living room, and always gave me the thinnest currant bread and tea when I visited them. They always had a small circlet of muslin hung with tiny coloured beads hung over the china milk jug on the tea table. Old Mr. Wheeldon made me a wheelbarrow when I was three, and he used to grow his own tobacco for his pipe. Dove Cottage was originally the living place for the old corn mill at Glutton Bridge, and the artist Harold Riley now has it.

   camel; *"It is easier for the camel to go through the eye of a needle, than for a rich man to enter the kingdom of God."* St. Mark, ch.10, v.25.

133 Echoes - from the past.

   susurrus; the whispering, rustling, sibilant sound synonymous with the rapid beating of birds' wings in flight.

134- ...and death?... - for me.

   death; I thought I'd get to grips with death now, rather than wait, and not be ready. I purposely spell '*death*' without a capital as it is relatively fairly unimportant in the grand scheme of things. Life being much more important.

135 Jigsaw - (*reprise*) - the last piece? ...or entropy on the arrow of time?

   gnomon; the rod, pin or pointer on the top of a sundial which indicates the time by the position of the shadow caused by it.

- *References* -

Ball, **Sir Christopher,** pgs 5, 12, 13 and back cover; the life and achievements of this gentleman are well documented: Educated at St. Georges School, Harpenden, later serving in the Parachute Regiment as a Second Lieutenant, he read English at Merton College gaining a first class degree. After lecturing in Oxford, he moved to be a tutor in comparative linguistics at the School of Oriental and African Studies, a part of the University of London. He returned to the University of Oxford as a Fellow and lecturer in English at Lincoln College, also serving as Bursar. Later he was appointed Warden of Keble College, being knighted for his services in Education in 1988. He was appointed an Honorary Fellow of Lincoln College in 1981, Merton College in 1987 and of Keble College in 1989. He was Chancellor of Derby University from 1995 to 2003 and has written many acclaimed works on educational and linguistic matters, also poetry under his pen name, John Elinger. He is well known for his fund-raising and charitable works and has the honour of being nominated for the Guinness Book of Records for his outstanding marathon running feats.

Derbyshire dialect - examples occur on pgs: 18, 23, 64, 89, 101, 110, 121, 124, 125, 126, 140, 143, 146, 149, 150 & 151. For the dialect enthusiast two books may be recommend: *"Two Collections of Derbicisms"* by Samuel Pegge, A.M., written in the last half of the 18th century, published in 1896 by Thomas Hallam for The English Dialect Society by O.U.P..
Or: *"Words of the White Peak – The Disappearing Dialect of a Derbyshire Village."* F. Philip Holland, ISBN 9781898670155, published in 2008.
        One of the earliest English writers to mention Derbyshire dialect was Philip Kinder. He wrote in his *Prolusion* to his *'Booke of Darbieshire'*:
        'They have no thunder in their speech, or crashing of the teeth, like the lower Britons in France; they speak not in the throat like the Welch; they have no querolous tone like the Irish, no grave tone descending in the fall like the Scotch, no wharlting like them of Carleton in Leicestershire, but something a broad language like the Dorick dialect in Greek' P. Kinder.

Elinger, John, p 5; b. 1935 and lives in Oxford. He has recently published two Collections of poems: "*Still Life*" & "*Operatic Interludes*". In 2009 he won first prize in the Local Poems competition with *'The Cooling Towers of Didcot'*, and was Visiting Poet at the University of Augusta, Georgia. His next Collection,

151

"*The Sights of Oxford*", (with illustrations by Katharine Shock) will appear in 2013. John Elinger is the pen name used by Sir Christopher John Elinger Ball when writing poetry.

Elkin, Roger, pgs 7, 8, & 9 ; poet, lecturer, and literary critic. He was born in Biddulph, Staffordshire, and has been at the forefront of the world of poetry and literature for many years; as an editor of poetry periodicals; as a university tutor; a respected judge of poetry competitions; a well-known published poet of many anthologies; an evergreen winner of poetry prizes and a much respected commentator on all matters literary. He has won well over 100 prizes (34 first prizes) in national and international poetry events, his critical essays have been published in many journals and he was the editor of *'Envoi'* for many years.

Kinder, Philip, pg 10; b.1597 – d. in, or after, 1665. Writer, Physician, Poet and Royalist, he was the second son of William Kinder, (c.1540 – d.1623.) who graduated from Brasenose College, Oxford, with a degree in Medicine. Philip chose the same profession as his father, graduating from Pembroke College, Cambridge, in 1616, with a licence to practise Medicine, apparently following Paracelsian principles. In 1629 he received an annuity of £20 p.a. from the Pierreponts, a powerful family in Nottingham. In 1640, Kinder, a staunch Royalist, was with the King's army at York. He completed a detailed survey of the monuments in York Minster, but the manuscript was lost at Nottingham in 1643. At the outbreak of the Civil War, the Royalist cavalry commander, Henry Hastings, appointed Kinder to be his agent at the Oxford court, and he was in the garrison of Ashby castle when it fell to the Parliamentarians in 1646. Kinder wrote Latin, studied Greek and Hebrew, and understood Spanish and Italian. His eclectic writings include some accomplished verse as well as prose, drama, topography, genealogy, astrology and literary criticism. By 1661 he was living near Melbourne, in Derbyshire. Later he lived at Walton-on-Trent, where he began and consolidated his epistolary friendship with Charles Cotton. Cotton encouraged him to write his best known work; the project for a *"Historie of Darby-shire"*(1663). Kinder's *'Booke'* and other works are mainly housed in Duke Humfrey's Library, Oxford, (Ashmole 788), with some transcriptions and other notes held within the 'Gell Papers', in the Derbyshire Archival Library, Matlock, Derbyshire.
(Author's note; Whilst studying his writings, both at Oxford and Matlock, I was delighted to discover he had faithfully recorded our shared Kinder family tree from 1385 to his latter years around 1660.)

- *Publication & Performance* -

"*Selected Poems*" (2004),
"*More Poems*" (2005)
"*Poetry Times Three*" (2006),
"*Fourth in Line*" (2007)
"*Words of the White Peak*", *(*2008) ISBN 9781898670155
"*Words of a Derbyshire Poet*" (2009) ISBN 9781906722128
"Jigsaw" (2012) ISBN 9780957361904

"*The Girl with Auburn Hair*" and "*Once*" were both exhibited in 'The Oxo Tower' and 'The Bargehouse', on the South Bank, in the London Art Co.'s '*Art of Love*' Competition, 2004.

"*The Coot*" was published in The Derbyshire County Community Anthology, "*Arnemetiae*", 2005.

"*Four*" was published in the Norwich Writers' Circle Open Poetry Competition's Anthology, 2007.

"*The Gather*" won Joint First Prize in The Huddersfield Literary Festival's Open Poetry Competition in March, 2007 and was also published in "*The North*" Poetry Magazine, June Edition, 2007.

"Foxfire" was Commended in the Wirral Festival of Firsts Open Poetry Competition, 2012.

Numerous other poems have been published in; '*Derbyshire Life & Countryside*', '*Country Images*' and '*Reflections*' magazines, and in '*Verbal Hedonists*' and '*Writer's Reign*' anthologies for Derby University.

The author performed at: The Buxton Festival Fringe 2004 – 2009; The Edinburgh Festival Fringe 2005; Buxton Festival Literary Series 2010; Ashbourne Arts Festival 2011; The Buxton Festival 2010 & 2011; Chester Festival 2011 & 2012; Leek Arts Festival 2011 & 2012; appeared on B.B.C. North West News, Manchester Evening News Channel 'M'; read his poetry on B.B.C. Radio Sheffield, B.B.C. Radio Derby, High Peak Radio, and Erewash Radio, and has given many recitals at all kinds of Societies, Clubs and Organisations in the Midlands and North West.

- Reviews & Data -

"Now we can begin to see the development of his own authentic voice speaking about the things which interest him; the countryside, as expected from someone who has spent the greater part of his life farming; music, as also expected from a fine musician, but other sources as well, ranging from a pair of curtains to a pair of rhinos in South Africa. Philip reads his poetry with a quiet confidence which is most attractive. The addition of musical excerpts introducing and closing the poems, and sometimes between the verses, serves to point up the particular quality of each poem and heightens our enjoyment."

Peter Low, 2005

"Philip's poetry is quarried from his Derbyshire and flows with the unconscious, natural speech rhythms and dialect of this locality. The theme of natural change is celebrated with a sense of security about our place in time, using contemplative, perceptive poems that make you respond with a wry smile of recognition, or laugh out loud with shared appreciation and understanding. The diversity of the poetry is entertaining: an amusing allegorical free verse about the life of a pair of shoes; a parody of a rhyming poem John Betjeman might have penned on a wet High Street; to my personal favourite, "The Gather", a poem that works like a riddle and is full of the fresh voice of a new poet sharing a moment of heightened emotion."

Alyson Phillips, 2007

"His work is not confined to the countryside however. His interests extend in many directions including the Holocaust, a brace of sonnets, the appearance and rapid disappearance of new restaurants and a particularly nostalgic account of Buxton Market in 1913. This is not all. Amongst his talents Philip is also an

*accomplished pianist and he uses the piano most effectively to set
different scenes for the verses. His choice of music to suit the mood
of the poem which followed essentially a personal one, but
nevertheless always heightened interest in the poetry."*

Peter Low, 2008

*"Philip Holland delivers, with feeling and gusto, a rich
variety of poetry in differing styles, structure and content, from the
serious to the silly. There was something to please everyone whether
it be to provoke a smile or make you ponder, interspersed with
appropriate snippets of well played piano pieces. There was love,
tragedy, dialect, animals, and the weather drawn from life's
experiences, which I was able to relate to immediately. Simple titles
belied the depth of observation of their author. Recommended
whether you know Philip's poetry or not, you simply must hear a
'disappearing poem' of what happened on the wedding night of two
three-toed sloths!"*

Nicola Stacey, 2009

"Words of the White Peak" (2008) ISBN 9781898670155:

Featured on B.B.C. Radio 4 in the '*Today*' programme with
John Humphrys, B.B.C. Radio 5, B.B.C. East Midlands T.V., B.B.C.
North West T.V., Manchester Evening News Channel 'M' T.V.,
Smooth Radio, Radio Derby, High Peak Radio and Erewash Sound.

Extracts from:
> *"The Earl Sterndale Dialect Poems of F. Philip Holland"*
> by Michael Robert Le-Baigue, University of Sheffield.

'Philip Holland is best described as multi-talented and not
your average farmer. His publication *"Words of the White Peak",
2008,* is a clever dialect dictionary, a mixture of academia and

creative writing which formed part of his B.A.Hons. study of the dialect around Earl Sterndale. Holland interviewed long-established inhabitants of his local area and explains he also drew on his: *"...own experience and memory of hearing, knowing and speaking this dialect in everyday life as a farmer."*

He was inspired to write this dialect dictionary as a record of his life and occupation and to: *"...hopefully serve to illustrate all the seasons, sights, sounds, smells, tastes and touches, bringing an awareness of the daily round of work and play, and share a few moments in the life and times of a hill-farmer."*

The concern Holland has with dialect disappearance is best summed up by her Grace the Dowager Duchess of Devonshire in her Foreword to the book:

"This book has been written just in time. The richness of a fast-disappearing vocabulary in what was once a remote area of the High Peak is very fascinating to people who are only accustomed to voices heard on radio and television. How many remember hand-milking, hoeing, ploughing with one horse, its harness, stabling and all that was familiar before mechanisation? The crops, the work in the garden, the domestic details of coal-fired kitchen ranges are of another world. It is wonderful that the result's of F. Philip Holland's research and memories have been collected in this book to remind us of what has gone before."
Deborah, Dowager Duchess of Devonshire, 2008.

Holland's pledge is to try and offset this decline, or if all else fails, at least have a record of the words which were once used locally. His dialect poetry intentionally evokes an authenticity which is generated from his local genealogy and a 'sense of place' which comes from his experienced lifetime as a hill-farmer in the four High Peak hills around Glutton Grange.'
Michael Robert Le Baigue, 2010

"*Words of a Derbyshire Poet*" (2009) ISBN 9781906722128:

"Philip Holland is obviously a poet of place and also of people...For this poet, it almost seems that the life of nature is as full of character and interest, and as intimately known and cherished, as the humans he writes about...The author's range is remarkable...
These poems demonstrate an astonishing variety of topics, genres and forms...His nature poems are superb, revealing the keen eye and ear of the countryman, and the farmer's affectionate familiarity with plants and animals...These poems need to be read more than once if they are to yield up their full value..."

Sir Christopher Ball, 2009

"This is a generous collection: nearly 150 pieces (poems, ballads, stories, and observations) ranging from Europe to the Middle East, South Africa to New Zealand, and featuring a range of people, both historical and fictional, from Hannibal to Henry VIII, and D. H. Lawrence to Harry Potter."
"However, its real heart is much closer to home: the landscape, its flora and fauna, and the hill-farmers of the Peak District of Derbyshire, their work, traditions, history and memories. Philip Holland brings together all his attributes from his life's experiences; as a former hotelier, he knows the need to make people feel at home, comfortable, at ease: as a classically-trained concert pianist, he is aware of the subtleties of music, its nuances, gentle rhythms, its sudden contrasts via change of tone or discord; as a handler of jewellery he knows the delights of the many-faceted, the play of light, the brilliance of special gems; but above all, as a country-lad brought up on a farm, he has a close empathy and sensitivity with the natural world."
"Holland's writing exhibits all these attributes and more: warm, accessible, memorable, musical – this is a gem of a collection from someone for whom words are important and who knows how to use them successfully in the sharing of his world."

Roger Elkin, 2009

- Epilogue -

"When images, senses, thoughts and memories are unclear, when the present is incomprehensible, and when the future is impenetrable; then words written in poetry can invoke and set free those feelings which are often difficult to express in everyday language."

F. Philip Holland

- Addendum -

The author is available to give Poetry Readings and Recitals, punctuated with live piano music, for all kinds of Festivals, Societies, Organisations, Clubs and private functions.

Please inquire:

email: philipholland@uwclub.net ,
Work: 01298 71938

All books by the author are available directly from:

Five-Bar-Gate Publishing,
1. Moorcroft, Lismore Road, Buxton,
Derbyshire, SK17 9GA
01298 27644

or Mayfield Books & Gifts,
9. Orgreave Close, Handsworth, Sheffield, S13 9NP
01142 889 522,

Prices for all books - quantities and postage - on request.

For further information:
Google: F. Philip Holland, Derbyshire Poet
Blog: f.philipholland@gmail .com
www.fphiliphollandpoetry.co.uk

P.Holland